Perceiving
Behaving
Becoming

Lessons Learned

Edited by H. Jerome Freiberg

Association for Supervision
and Curriculum Development

Alexandria, Virginia USA

Association for Supervision and Curriculum Development
1703 N. Beauregard St. • Alexandria, VA 22311-1714 USA
Telephone: 1-800-933-2723 or 703-578-9600 • Fax: 703-575-5400
Web site: http://www.ascd.org • E-mail: member@ascd.org

Gene R. Carter, *Executive Director*
Michelle Terry, *Associate Executive Director, Program Development*
Nancy Modrak, *Director, Publishing*
John O'Neil, *Director of Acquisitions*
Julie Houtz, *Managing Editor of Books*
Jo Ann Irick Jones, *Senior Associate Editor*
Carolyn R. Pool, *Associate Editor*
Charles D. Halverson, *Project Assistant*
Gary Bloom, *Director, Design and Production Services*
Eva Barsin, *Senior Designer*
Tracey A. Smith, *Production Manager*
Dina Murray, *Production Coordinator*
John Franklin, *Production Coordinator*
Valerie Sprague, *Desktop Publisher*

Printed in the United States of America.

s3/99

ASCD Stock No.: 199031
ASCD member price: $16.95   nonmember price: $20.95

Library of Congress Cataloging-in-Publication Data
Perceiving, behaving, becoming : lessons learned / H. Jerome
Freiberg, editor.
    p. cm.
    Includes bibliographical references
    ISBN 0-87120-341-3
    1. Education—Aims and objectives—United States. 2. Educational
psychology—United States. 3. Affective education—United States.
4. Education, Humanistic—United States. 5. Yearbook (Association
for Supervision and Curriculum Development). I. Freiberg, H. Jerome.
    LA217.2 .P45 1999
    370.15—dc21   98-58125
                                                              CIP

03 02 01 00 99   5 4 3 2 1

Perceiving, Behaving, Becoming: Lessons Learned

Acknowledgments

I am indebted to many people for their assistance in creating this book, including Ruth Silva for her able organization and proofing skills and to Saundra McNeese for her administrative support in completing this book.

Perceiving, Behaving, Becoming: Lessons Learned would not be possible without the expertise, assistance, and support of the ASCD team, including Jo Ann Jones, John O'Neil, Nancy Modrak, Julie Houtz, and Ron Brandt, who initiated the book project.

This book was made possible by the dedication of the response authors, who agreed to take on a challenging task and provide the readership of ASCD and others the opportunity to see a classic work reprinted within the context of a new millennium.

Introduction

H. Jerome Freiberg

LESSONS LEARNED

There comes a time when present generations need to have a reminder of the past, for the past shapes the future. *Perceiving, Behaving, Becoming: A New Focus for Education*, ASCD's 1962 Yearbook, was the culmination of decades of thinking and debate about what the new era of living should be. Earl C. Kelley, Carl R. Rogers, Abraham H. Maslow, and Arthur W. Combs, preeminent psychologists, were invited by ASCD to prepare papers that would become the heart of the 1962 Yearbook. Their works make up the first part of the book. The 19 members of the Yearbook Committee wrote Chapters 6–15. The goal of *Perceiving, Behaving, Becoming: A New Focus for Education* is stated in the first page:

> It may seem paradoxical to say that *Perceiving, Behaving, Becoming: A New Focus for Education* is timely. How can it be timely in a period in which attention in education is riveted on the technological revolution, alternative proposals for organizational structures, and updating knowledge in government-favored academic areas? *Perceiving, Behaving, Becoming* is timely precisely because continuous consideration of the basic foundations of the educational program is inescapable. Regardless of what technological devices are adopted, what organizational patterns prevail, what curriculum content emerges, the three basic foundations of education—social, psychological and philosophical—are central in the making of the educational program.

Essentially, the 1962 Yearbook of the Association for Supervision and Curriculum Development provides bold new insight on one of the three foundations, the psychological, with related implications affecting social and philosophical aspects. *Perceiving, Behaving, Becoming* deals with the truly adequate person, adequate in the sense of Webster's synonym *sufficient* and in the sense of the authors' equivalent phrases, *fully functioning* and *self-actualizing*, rather than adequate in the corrupted usage, "good enough to get by." The yearbook describes how schools may help develop such persons.

Here is no trivial contribution by scholars avoiding reality; here the authors deal with the heart of the educational process as they propose a new focus for education. If they prove to be correct in their espousal of a "third force" in psychology, neither behavioristic nor Freudian, a hopeful vista as to man's potentiality stretches ahead. The theories and applications of *Perceiving, Behaving, Becoming* merit intent and open-minded study by the reader. (ASCD, 1962, p. iii)

In 1962, many who are reading this volume were not born; others were in grade school or high school. However, a few people were already shaping the future by their actions in the '30s, '40s, '50s, and '60s. Earl Kelley, Carl Rogers, Abraham Maslow, and Art Combs were creating new paradigms of thinking long before the term came into vogue. They built their ideas from Kurt Lewin, John Dewey, and centuries of debate about the nature of learning. They recoiled against the predestined ideologies of the behavioral theories of Watson, Pavlov, and others who ruled in the 1940s and 1950s. They gave a voice to people who were seeking another way to explain learning and teaching and the importance of the individual in the equation of life.

THE '60s: A TIME OF TRANSFORMATION

It may help in reading works from the 1960s to have a context for the writings. The 1960s were a time of social, political, and class transformation. Women and people of color were seeking, obtaining, and achieving their places in the job market and in colleges and universities. They were also obtaining jobs in fields where opportunities had been limited or nonexistent in the past. That people be judged by their ability rather than the color of their skin, or their gender, was a rallying cry of Martin Luther King and others of the Civil Rights Movement. From the grass roots to Presidents John F. Kennedy and Lyndon Johnson, people came to see a vision of America that was much more inclusive from that of the previous 200 years.

The United States emerged from the second world war as an economic powerhouse and the keeper of democracy and freedom. The returning soldiers were rewarded with the GI Bill, which gave low-interest home loans and free higher education. For the first time lower-class youth of all races had the resources to attend higher education and achieve a higher quality of life. The end of World War II brought hope, prosperity, and children. Those born between 1945 and 1965 formed new generations of children labeled by the media as the "baby boomers"; they crowded into schools and classrooms by the millions. It was a time when "drive by" was a term used by real estate agents, when Bill Gates was thinking about what could be, and Apple was still the name of a fruit. It is into this context that *Perceiving, Behaving, Becoming: A New Focus for Education* was originally published.

The '60s were about change. Educational change parallels the flow of waves in the ocean. The first wave begins to form a swell far from the shoreline. It then reaches a crest and finally breaks on the shore. While the first wave is reaching its crest a second wave is beginning to form. The cycle then repeats itself. The progressive movement advanced by the works of John Dewey and others was reaching its peak in the early 1940s, just as the United States was entering World War II. It was during, and shortly after the war, that the behavioristic movement led by B. F. Skinner and its application to education using teaching machines and behavioral classroom discipline were at its peak. A new wave was forming—the humanistic movement or the "third force" in psychology, "neither behavioristic nor Freudian," which was led by the original four authors of this text and built on human potential of the individual. Third force psychology furthered the development of the humanistic education movement in the 1960s and 1970s.

The humanistic movement focuses on the potential of the individual. The leadership of the movement came from psychology; it remained for others to translate the theories into educational practice. Little research was conducted during the '60s and '70s, and what research was available was not published in easily accessible publications. Publications like *Educational Leadership* and *Phi Delta Kappan* in the 1960s had few references to the research or evaluation of programs or projects that adhered to the philosophies of Kelley, Rogers, Maslow, or Combs. Generally, much of what existed became activity-centered books for the classroom (e.g., Values

Clarification, 101 Ways to Motivate Students). It was easy then for even flawed research to scuttle potentially effective ideas.

The classic case in point is the demise of open education. In a synthesis of studies of open education, Walberg, in the *Handbook of Research on Teaching* (1986), reviewed the works of researchers who themselves reviewed hundreds of studies on open education (Horwitz, 1979; Peterson, 1979; and Hedges, Giaconia, & Gage, 1981). He found the following:

> Despite the differences in study selection and methods, the three syntheses, which cover more or less substantial parts of the corpus of research, converge roughly on the same plausible conclusion: Students in open classes do slightly or no worse in standardized achievement and slightly to substantially better on several outcomes that educators, parents, and students hold to be of great value. Unfortunately, the negative conclusion of Bennett's (1976) single study—introduced by a prominent psychologist, published by Harvard University Press, publicized by the *New York Times* and by experts that take that newspaper as their source—probably sounded the death knell of open education, even though the conclusion of the study was later retracted (Aitken, Bennett, & Hesketh, 1981) because of obvious statistical flaws in the original analysis (Aitken, Anderson, & Hinde, 1981). (Walberg 1986, p. 226)

EDUCATIONAL RESEARCH

The issue of research was a concern for Carl Rogers after the publication of *Freedom to Learn* for the '80s; when we met in 1984 he said, "I feel it's very necessary to not simply issue a statement [about education] but to back your statements with research. . . ." He was concerned by the fact that too many important educational experiences and ideas were being "thrown out" without careful consideration. Research to him was not only numbers, but included the systematic collection of ideas and experiences to form trends, patterns, directions, and case studies upon which new learnings could be built. Parenthetically, during several sessions at the 1987 national meeting of the American Educational Research Association, leading educational researchers suggested the use of case studies and other one-to-one strategies for collecting in-depth information to build new knowledge and understanding about teaching and learning. These early beginnings for case knowledge and qualitative understandings have blossomed into a field of educational research that has paralleled quantitative research.

Longitudinal studies of humanistic teaching conducted in the Philadelphia schools indicated that students who participated in the programs "achieved at statistically significant levels on standardized reading tests; they also persist longer on reading tasks and write more completely and complexly than do comparison groups" (Newberg, 1980). Aspy and Roebuck (1977) conducted studies with 10,000 students and teachers on the types of relationships that occur in schools. They found the following:

1. Teachers' levels of Empathy (E), Congruence (C), and Unconditional Positive Regard (UPR) are positively and significantly related to
   • Students' cognitive growth
   • Students' IQ gains
   • Students' attendance

2. Teachers' present levels of interpersonal functioning (E, C, and UPR) are generally below those required for minimal facilitation of student growth.

3. Teachers can enhance and promote their levels of interpersonal functioning (E, C, and UPR) through systematic skills training.

4. Teachers' gains in the interpersonal dimensions (E, C, and UPR) are translated into positive gains by their students.

WHY AN UPDATE?

Education is clearly more than facts, information, and skills; it requires a sense of what was, a sense of what is, and a vision that will allow us to project what might be. Education directly affects the future and is built on the past (Houston, Clift, Freiberg, & Warner, 1988, p. 22). This revision of *Perceiving, Behaving, Becoming* will give a reality check to what was proposed to improve the quality of education nearly 40 years ago.

Can a book written halfway through the 20th century have any relevance for educators starting the new millennium of the 21st century? Once you read this book, you will see the significance of the work for contemporary efforts to transform and renew education.

This revision had its beginnings in 1996, when I met with Ron Brandt at the American Educational Research Association to discuss possible projects for ASCD. He asked if I would be interested in updating *Perceiving, Behaving, Becoming: A New Focus for Education*, which was out of print. He also stated it would need to be a labor of love, in that ASCD could provide no compensation or financial assistance to me or others for the revision. I agreed to revise it and to write a response to Carl Rogers' chapter. Each of the original four chapters would be reprinted as in the 1962 edition, accompanied by responses.

In 1994 I had revised *Freedom to Learn* into a third edition. I had worked with Carl Rogers on the second edition of his book. During this time I was the president of the Affective Special Interest Group of the American Educational Research Association. I have devoted my adult life to children who are underserved by society and our educational system. Currently I am working through the Consistency Management & Cooperative Discipline Project to implement whole school reform efforts with inner-city schools in Houston, Chicago, and Newark.

In preparing the revision of *Perceiving, Behaving, Becoming*, I asked leading scholars who have had significant influence in the field of affective/humanistic education and psychology to respond to the original four chapters. Policymakers today have a bleak view of the humanistic movement from the '60s and '70s. They have associated humanism with permissiveness and freedom with license. Ron Brandt and I felt that a review of the writings of Earl C. Kelley, Carl R. Rogers, Abraham H. Maslow, and Arthur W. Combs would provide a context for lessons learned for future generations of educators.

The revision departs from the original in two significant ways: First, I did not think an uncritical look at the original four chapters would work, nor be very meaningful for today's reader. Second, each chapter needed a direct response rather than a global view. Many of the responding authors are affiliated with universities, but in each case they work with teachers, administrators, and schools and have a unique perspective on the human side of teaching and learning:

1. Earl Kelley's "The Fully Functioning Self"
- *Norm Newberg*, University of Pennsylvania, Philadelphia, Pennsylvania
  - *Mary Sudzina*, University of Dayton, Dayton, Ohio

2. Carl Rogers' "Toward Becoming a Fully Functioning Person"
- *H. Jerome Freiberg*, University of Houston, Houston, Texas
- *Dottie Bonner*, Austin High School, Houston, Texas
- *Lawrence Kohn*, Quest High School, Humble, Texas
- *Carolyn Jackson*, Scarborough High School, Houston, Texas

3. Abraham Maslow's "Some Basic Propositions of a Growth and Self-Actualization Psychology"
- *Alfie Kohn*, an author, writer, and educational consultant, Belmont, Massachusetts
- *Dolf van Veen*, Hogeschool van Amsterdam, The Netherlands, and *Christopher Day* of the University of Nottingham in England

4. Arthur Combs's "A Perceptual View of the Adequate Personality"
- *Hermine Marshall*, San Francisco State University, San Francisco, California
- *Barbara McCombs*, Mid-continent Regional Educational Laboratory, Aurora, Colorado

THE TRANSFER OF KNOWLEDGE

The updated version gives a context to ideas developed in 1962. The fact that race and gender issues of the time were ignored in some of the original chapters needs to be said. The 1962 edition was written between 1960–62, from six to eight years after Brown v. the Board of Education, Topeka (1954), in which the U.S. Supreme Court ruled that segregated schools ("separate but equal") are unconstitutional. The fact that Maslow's work may be misused in the '90s, or that his theory of a hierarchy of needs has not met the research standards of today, also needs to be said. But Maslow's way of conceptualizing the basic needs of people stimulated the debate and subsequent government support for free and reduced lunch school programs for children of poverty more than 30 years ago. A critical analysis format of the period and lessons learned for today will go further in advancing the cause of person-centered education than a general overview of the chapters. Therefore, the revised edition is entitled: *Perceiving, Behaving, Becoming: Lessons Learned.*

Society establishes institutions to reflect its values and beliefs in the hope that these cultural elements will transfer to the next generation. Schools today have evolved from schools of the past, and the ideas and commitments of educational leaders, and societal movements and counter movements. *Perceiving, Behaving, Becoming: Lessons Learned* provides an important lesson for the future. I conclude this section with a passage from the 1962 text:

> We cannot predict the world of 2015 when today's kindergartners will be dealing with a very different world of ideas, people, and processes. We cannot know which bits of present information will be needed in that world. We can be very certain, however, that providing schools which facilitate the development of persons with adequate, fully functioning personalities is the best way to contribute some degree of stability to an uncertain future. The person who has a positive view of self, who is open to experience, who is creative, who is trustworthy and responsible, who has values, who is well informed, and who is aware that he [or she] is in the process of becoming is the person most able to survive and deal with the future. What is more, he [or she] will do a better job for the rest of us (p. 253).

*   *   *

Education is a human endeavor, and the need to create learning environments that respond to changing learner needs will be a continuous process. Civilizations rise and fall on the ability of the society to transfer knowledge gained from past and present generations to future generations. Along with the ancient technological advances of fire, tools, bronze, steel, the wheel, and farming came advances in teaching these "new" technologies to others. A breakdown in the educational system—no matter how crude—clearly indicates the demise of the civilization. Schools reflect the ills of society, and yet the school can be a place in which these ills can be corrected for future generations (Houston, Clift, Freiberg, & Warner,

p. 22). I hope you find a better sense of our educational future by seeing the evolution of our past.

References

Aitken, M., Anderson, D., & Hinde, J. (1981). Modeling of data on teaching styles [With discussion]. *Journal of the Royal Statistical Society* (series A), pp. 144, 419–461.

Aitken, M. Bennett, S. N., & Hesketh, J. (1981). Teaching styles and pupil progress: A re-analysis. *British Journal of Educational Psychology, 51*, Part 2, 170–186.

Aspy, N., & Roebuck, F. N. (1977). *Kids don't learn from people they don't like.* Amherst, MA: Human Resource Development Press.

Bennett, S. N. (1976). *Teaching styles and pupil progress.* Shepton Mallet, Somerset, England: Open Books.

Combs, A. W. (Ed.). (1962). *Perceiving, behaving, becoming: A new focus for education.* 1962 ASCD yearbook. Alexandria, VA: Association for Supervision and Curriculum Development.

Hedges, L. V., Giaconia, R. M., & Gage, N. L. (1981). *Meta-analysis of the effect of open and traditional instruction.* Stanford University, Program on Teaching Effectiveness, Stanford, CA.

Horwitz, R. A. (1979). Psychological effects of the open classroom. *Review of Educational Research, 49*(1), 71–85.

Houston, W. R., Clift, R. T., Freiberg, H. J., and Warner, A. (1988). *Touch the future–Teach.* St. Paul, MN: West Publishing Co.

Newberg, N. (1980, April 7–11). Affective education: Address the basics. Paper presented at the National Meeting of the American Educational Research Association, Boston, Massachusetts.

Peterson, P. L. (1979). Direct instruction reconsidered. In P. L. Peterson & H. J. Walberg (Eds.), *Research on teaching.* Berkeley, CA: McCutchan.

Rogers, C. R., and Freiberg, H. J. (1994). *Freedom to learn.* 3rd ed. Columbus: Merrill.

Walberg, H. (1986). Synthesis of research on teaching. In M. Wittrock (Ed.), *Handbook of research on teaching* (3rd ed.). New York: Macmillan.

The Fully Functioning Self

Earl C. Kelley

This chapter originally appeared in the 1962 ASCD Yearbook, *Perceiving, Behaving, Becoming: A New Focus for Education*.

From the 1962 ASCD Yearbook

The Fully Functioning Self

Earl C. Kelley • *Wayne State University*

In a discussion of the self, it will perhaps be helpful to attempt to say as well as we can what it is we are trying to discuss. This is done at the risk of using the conversation stopper, "Let's define it." Many a fine discussion has ended at this point.

The self consists, in part at least, of the accumulated experiential background, or backlog, of the individual. It is what has been built, since his life began, through unique experience and unique purpose, on the individual's unique biological structure. The self is therefore unique to the individual.

This self is built almost entirely, if not entirely, in relationship to others. While the newborn babe has the equipment for the development of the self, there is ample evidence to show that nothing resembling a self can be built in the absence of others. Having a cortex is not enough; there must be continuous interchange between the individual and others. Language, for example, would not be possible without social relationships. Thus, it is seen that man is necessarily a social being.

The self has to be achieved; it is not given. All that is given is the equipment and at least the minimal (mother and child) social environment. Since the self is achieved through social contact, it has to be understood in terms of others. "Self and other" is not a duality, because they go so together that separation is quite impossible.

The self consists of an organization of accumulated experience over a whole lifetime. It is easy to see, therefore, that a great deal of the self has been relegated to the unconscious, or has been "forgotten." This does not mean that these early experiences have been lost. It merely means that they cannot readily be brought into consciousness. We must recognize the fact that the unconscious part of the self functions, for weal or woe, depending on the quality of the experiences.

It is intended here, however, to deal with the conscious self. The unconscious self (not a separation but a continuum) is difficult to deal with for the very reason that it is below the level of consciousness. We want here to look especially at how the individual sees himself. This is indeed the critical point, because it is what the person *sees* that is enabling or disabling. The crucial matter is not so much what you are, but what you think you are. And all of this is always in relationship to others.

The fully functioning personality (self) needs to have certain characteristics. Here, perhaps, is as good a place as any to discuss word trouble. We live in a moving, changing, becoming-but-never-arriving world, yet our language was built by people who believed this to be a static world. I have often spoken of the adequate self, but "adequate" will not do, because it is static. In fact, "inadequate" is a more useful word than "adequate." If there were a word that combines "aspiring-becoming," it would come close to our needs. I have chosen "fully functioning," which I think I learned from Carl Rogers, as the best I can do. This expression at least implies movement.

In order for a person to be fully functioning, when he looks at his self, as he must, he must see that it is enough—enough to perform the task at hand. He must see in his experiential background some history of success. He needs to see process, the building and becoming nature of himself. This being so, he will see that today has no meaning in the absence of yesterdays and tomorrows. In fact, there could be no today except for both yesterday and tomorrow. He must like what he sees, at least well enough for it to be operational.

MANY PEOPLE DO NOT LIKE THEIR SELVES

Unfortunately, many people in the world today suffer from inadequate concepts of self, which naturally lead to mistaken notions of others. Perhaps everybody is afflicted thus to some degree. There may be some rare spirits who are not, but they are few indeed.

We see evidence of this all around us. We see people ridden by unreasonable fears. The fearful person looks at his self and sees that it is not sufficient to meet what he fears. Middle-aged graduate students are afraid to stick their necks out. They are afraid to write; they suffer from stage fright. The question uppermost in their minds is, "What will people think?" Their selves are veritable skeletons in their closets, and if one has a skeleton in his closet, it is best not to do anything except to keep quiet. Any move may reveal it. So they try to sit tight so that they may not be revealed to others. This is a great loss to others—to mankind—for new paths are forbidding and exploration is fraught with terrors.

This Is Crippling

An inadequate concept of self, so common in our culture, is crippling to the individual. Our psychological selves may become crippled in much the same way as our physical selves may be crippled by disease or by an accident. They are the same, in effect, because each limits what we can do. When we see ourselves as inadequate, we lose our "can-ness." There becomes less and less that we can do.

Perhaps it is unfortunate that we cannot see the psychological self in the same way that we see the physical self. Our hearts go out to the physical cripple—we do not enter him in a foot race—but we expect the psychological cripple to step lively and meet all of the vicissitudes of life as though he were whole. Both kinds of cripples need therapy, though of different sorts. Many benefit by therapy, though all do not.

How Do We Get That Way?

Now we come to the question, "How do we get that way?" We get that way in the same way that a physical cripple does—by the lives we lead. Of course there are some cases of congenital defect, but if these were the only cripples we had, we would be fortunate indeed.

The newborn babe has enormous potential for health, but this health has to be built out of his experience with others. It has to be achieved, and it has to be achieved in relationship to others. The health potential then lies strictly in the quality of the people around him, since the infant, for many years to come, has, himself, no control over whom he will associate with.

Damage to the self, so disabling to so many of us, comes from the fact that we grow up in an authoritarian culture. While it is true that this is a democracy in governmental form, we have not achieved democracy in the home, the school, or the church. The fact that we have a democratically chosen president or governor has no effect upon the developing child. He is built by the people close to him, and he does not elect them. The people close to him, having themselves been crippled, know no better than to continue the process.

The evils of authoritarianism are more extensive than is ordinarily understood. It is easy to see on a grand scale, as when a Hitler gains power. We all abhor a Hitler, but we seem to think that tyranny in small doses or on a small scale is somehow good. All in all, it appears that small tyrants do more harm than grand ones. The small tyrant operates on the growing edge of the personality of the young.

The trouble with the tyrant is basically that he does not have any faith in anyone except himself. He gets that way by living with people who never had any faith in him. Of course he does not really have any faith in himself either, but he has longed for and striven for a position of power over others weaker than himself. Getting his concept of others from his concept of himself, he believes that nothing worthwhile will happen unless he forces it to happen.

Lack of faith in others—the feeling that one has to see to it that others, who are perverse by nature, do what they should—starts a chain reaction of evils, one piled upon another. The burden one bears when he feels that he must watch others and coerce them must be unbearable. And so it turns out to be, for the tyrant deprives himself of others, and grows in the direction of more loneliness and hostility.

From this we can see what happens to the newborn babe as he faces the tyrant. Of course, the tyrant loves his baby in such manner as he is able to love. But he still regards the infant as a "thing," naturally in need of correction. One might think that the very young would not know the difference. But there are ample data to show that even in the first few days after birth, the child knows the difference between being loved and being viewed as in need of coercion. He knows whether the parent is doing things *with* him or *to* him. And the personality at that stage must be tender.

After five or six years of the authoritarian home, the child goes to school. The school is a place inhabited by adults, and too often these adults hold adult concepts of what a child ought to be. These concepts are unverified by the study of children. Here he meets preconceived standards, grade levels, and all of the other paraphernalia of the adult-centered school. If he does not measure up to these standards, then obviously he is perverse and in need of coercion. The fact that these standards are not derived from the child, that there is nothing about them in the Bible, that they arise and reside only in the minds of adults, bothers the adults not at all. Thus, coercion and criticism become the daily fare, while the deviations in behavior brought about by the uniqueness of the personality are stopped. Conformity is the way to the good life, and the best way to conform is to withdraw. One cannot be unique and extend himself and still conform. His uniqueness will show. Shells look a great deal alike, and so if one crawls into his shell, his differences will not be so apparent.

In our authoritarian culture, many forces converge upon the young individual which have the effect of making him think less of himself. The church is one of these forces. The concept of guilt, with its imaginary burden of sin, cannot help one to think well of himself. Of course one can acquire these damaging concepts without getting them at church. But those who have salvation to dispense hold a powerful weapon. When one is made to feel unworthy, he is crippled in some degree, because he cannot do what he otherwise might.

There is a distinction here between the effects of religion and the effects of the church as often administered. It is not religion per se which makes one think ill of himself. It is the representatives of religion who use authoritarian methods to gain their ends. Likewise schooling or education can be expanding in their nature. It is that the representatives of the school—teachers and administrators—often have their own ends to be served, not those of their learners. They act from their own fears, which cause them to dampen and delimit the expanding personalities of their young, thus defeating the very purpose for their being.

Nor is it intended here to deny the need for standards. A fully functioning personality cannot operate without standards. Such standards are the basis for aspiration, the basis for the hope for tomorrow. But it is doubtful that extrinsic, materialistic standards can be successfully applied. Standards have to be the product of values held, and of the life that has been led. The better the quality of the life that has been experienced, the better the values held and the standards which result from these values. Standards will be unique—not the same for everyone—even as the experience from which they are derived has been unique. They will be in terms of other human beings.

BASIS FOR HEALTHY GROWTH

The dynamic which changes a speck of protoplasm into a fully functioning human being is growth. The questions, then, are: What does he grow on? What are the environmental conditions which feed him?

We need to consider that in growing up one is developing both his physical structure and his psychological structure. We are most familiar with the physical structure and are apt to think of that as growth. We know what the body needs to develop and that lack of development will result in physical crippling. We can identify the diseases of malnutrition and know that a man will not become truly a man in the best sense without an adequate supply of the required stuff of physical growth.

All of the time that the physical body is being developed, so also is the psychological self. The physical body fortunately stops growing after about 20 years. The psychological self, however, continues to grow throughout life. As the physical body has its own unique food requirements, so does the psychological self. This is a different kind of stuff, however, with a different point of intake. We feed the psychological self through the perceptive process. This is what comes into consciousness when stimuli from the environment impinge on the organism. It is the stuff of growth for the personality, and it builds attitudes, habits, and knowledge. The perceptive stuff of growth provides the experiential background from which we operate. This controls what we do with the body. The quality of the perceptive stuff of growth therefore determines the quality of the behavior of the individual.

It is necessary here to make clear the fact that the physical body and the psychological self do not constitute a duality, even though it is necessary to speak of them one at a time. The organism is unitary in its operation. There is no body apart from personality, no psychological self without a body to inhabit. What affects one affects all. But that does not prevent speaking of a part. Although we know that hand and foot, attitude, emotion, and habit are all one, we still can talk of the hand as having certain characteristics while the foot has others. Speaking of parts does not deny the unitary nature of the individual.

WE SELECT WHAT WE WILL PERCEIVE

Since in this paper we are primarily concerned with the development of the fully functioning self, we will discuss what feeds the self and how it is fed. As we have noted, perception is the stuff of growth for the psychological self. The perceptive process is the only avenue by which the self can be fed. Recent understandings as to the nature of this process have enabled us to see more clearly than before how the self is built.

One of the most revealing facts about perception is that it is *selective*. We do not see everything in our surroundings. There are thousands of co-incidences in the situation in which we find ourselves at any point of time. To perceive them all would cause pandemonium. We therefore *choose* that which the self feeds upon. The direction of the growth of the self depends upon those choices.

The choices seem to be on the basis of experience and unique purpose. We all have a background of experience upon which perception is in part based. We cannot see that which we have no experience to see. But experience is not enough to account for what happens, for there are many objects in our surroundings with which we have had experience, but which we do not perceive.

The additional element which appears to determine perceptive intake is purpose. There is ample evidence now to show that all living tissue is purposive, and, of course, in man this purpose is partly, but only partly, on the conscious level. In perception, purpose operates automatically most of the time. And so, just as we do not eat everything, our psychological selves are particular as to what they feed on. What they take in has to suit their purposes, and has to fit onto their past experiences.

ENHANCEMENT AND DEFENSE

The self "looks out" upon the surrounding scene largely in terms of its own enhancement or defense. It tends to extend in the direction of that which promises to make it better off. It withdraws from that which seems likely to endanger it. This is largely true throughout life and entirely true in the early stages when the self is being established—when "self" and "other" first come into being. Altruism is a highly sophisticated concept, and, if it is achieved at all, it comes late. It is the result of great understanding of the self-other interdependency.

THE SELF NEEDS BOUNDARIES

If the self is going to reach out toward facilitating factors and withdraw from endangering ones, it has to have something to reach out from, something to hide behind. It helps to understand this if we assume that the self has to have boundaries in much the same sense that the physical self has to have a skin. The self has certain things that it will let in, others that it will keep out. The boundaries are not, of course, physical—to be seen—but neither is the self. A physical concept, however, helps us to comprehend it. So if we can imagine a physical shell, or armor, necessary for the confinement of the self, we then can imagine how it functions.

Some kind of boundary—a selective screen—is therefore essential to the maintenance of the self. We could not manage the affairs of living without something of this kind. It follows that the nature of the environment, whether it is seen to be facilitating or endangering, will determine the permeability of this screen. That is, the more facilitating the environment, the less need for protection. The more endangering the environment, the greater need for protection. Thus, under adverse conditions, the screen develops into a shell, so that very little is admitted. When this process is continued over a long period of time, that which enabled us to be selective in our perception becomes almost impermeable.

Boundaries then become barriers. Protection becomes isolation. The self becomes a prisoner in its own fort. We have all seen persons off whom words or ideas seemed to bounce. They have built their barriers against other people so strong that they have become inaccessible. Since fear feeds on itself, especially when a person is in isolation, it has a tendency to extend itself beyond the people who are endangering, to include all people.

When the fearful person withdraws within his psychological shell, communication is shut off. It is just as difficult for such a person to give as it is for him to receive. The self then is denied that which it feeds on. The psychological self feeds on ideas, which come from other people. Without the stuff of growth, the self becomes less adequate, and the whole person loses its ability to do, to venture, to create. The individual comes to see himself as impoverished, but he is not able to do much about it by himself.

THE GOOD LIFE TO LIVE

Such a person, however, by having enhancing relationships with others, can break down some of the barriers which separate him from others. By good experiences, he can become less fearful and more open. This process, too, feeds on itself, and confidence can be built by the quality of his experience with others. Confidence opens the barriers so that the perceptive stuff of growth can again be received. He has to learn not to see others as threats, but as assets. Of course, this will not happen unless others cease to act toward him as threats. The parent or teacher who depends upon threats or other techniques of fear will not be able to open the self of one who is in his power.

Fortunate indeed, and not too common in this authoritarian culture, is the person who has had the opportunity to grow up with people whom he can see as facilitating. Most of us have to build our shell against others; and if we are to have fully functioning selves, we have to have experiences which will open these shells.

For the development of a fully functioning self, a person needs to have opportunity to live the life good to live. This life, or his world, needs to be populated by people whom he can view as facilitating. It is almost entirely a matter of people, not things. Facilitating people can be poor in material things. In fact, some of the happiest and most open people are found in poor material circumstances. The most closed and fearful people, the most authoritarian people, may be surfeited by the material goods of the earth. While this is no plea for poverty and privation, it seems that the very possession of great quantities of material goods is apt by its very nature to make the holder fearful that he will lose his goods to others. Vague fear always causes the personality to close up and to become less accessible.

The life good to live does not depend upon the material status of the person. It depends upon the quality of the people around him. He needs people who are open, so that he can feel their quality. He needs people who respect him as a person from the very beginning. It is paradoxical that many parents love their young, but do not respect them. Parents and teachers often say that the child is, of course, too young to be able to make any decisions for himself. It is true that the newborn infant cannot make decisions. But the babe can feel the difference between being held in respect and being regarded as though he had no personality. Respect for the budding self brings it out. Disrespect starts the process of closing up, which in some of our older children and adults is often so complete.

The life good to live is a cooperative one. No child is too young to sense whether or not he lives in a cooperative relation with the people around him. The reason that cooperation is so important is that the cooperative atmosphere is one of involvement. The growing self must feel that it is involved, that it is really part of what is going on, that in some degree it is helping shape its own destiny, together with the destiny of all. Perhaps there is no one quality more important for the developing self than this feeling of involvement in what is taking place. This is what gives a person a "reason to be." The lack of consultation and involvement is the cause of the continuing war between parents and their children, between teachers and learners, between teachers and administrators, employers and employees, ad infinitum. When the person is a part of something, then he becomes responsible.

Whenever the cooperative life is proposed, the authoritarians say, "Oh yes, you want children (or workers or teachers) to do just as they please!" This is a gross misunderstanding of the cooperative way of life, and the shell on such people is so thick that we are baffled in our efforts to reach them. The fact is that in the cooperative life there is much less freedom "to do just as they please" than there is under the surveillance of the autocrat. For the obligation is owed, and the responsibility is felt, to ourselves and to those who facilitate us. The obligation is with us 24 hours a day, rather than just when the autocrat is looking. We do not neglect or sabotage our own projects. This happens to the other's project, particularly if he has met us with threat or fear.

The cooperative life, where everyone from his beginning receives the respect due to a person, and, as he is able, becomes involved in and responsible for what goes on, is not an easy life. The obligation is continuous and pressing. But the difficulties of such a life are inherent in the living, and they cause the self to extend and stretch and grow. These difficulties have quite the opposite effect from those thought up by and inflicted on us by someone else. The latter, not having meaning to the person, cause him to withdraw and begin to calculate how he can protect himself.

THE FULLY FUNCTIONING PERSON

What is a person with a fully functioning self like? This can be answered only in terms of his behavior. Conclusions can be drawn from this behavior. The temptation here is to vest this person, like Rose Aylmer, with "every virtue, every grace." Rather than simply listing virtues, there are some characteristics not necessarily cherished in our culture, which such a person would logically have. From what has been stated here, it might be inferred that nobody has escaped with a fully functioning self. And it seems to be likely that very few survive home, church, and school without damage to the self.

Yet there are a good many people who, through contact with facilitating persons, have been reopened and whose selves function well. To argue otherwise would be to deny the potential for change and improvement on which life itself depends. In fact, it can be considered that no one can experience elation who has never known despair; no one can be courageous without having known fear. So the human personality is not doomed to endure its present state, but can be brought into flower by enhancing experiences. As Karen Horney has said, "My own belief is that man has the capacity as well as the desire to develop his potentialities and become a decent human being, and that these deteriorate if his relationship to others and hence to himself is, and continues to be, disturbed. I believe that man can change and keep on changing as long as he lives" (Horney, 1945).

The fully functioning personality thinks well of himself. He looks at himself and likes what he sees well enough so that he can accept it. This is essential to doing, to "can-ness." He does not see himself as able to do anything and everything, but he sees himself as able in terms of his experience. He feels he can do what is reasonable to expect on the basis of his experience.

Those who do not like what they see when they look at themselves are the fearful ones—not just afraid of present danger, but taking a fearful view of everything in general. Fear renders them helpless, and this leads to alienation from others and hostility toward others, thus shutting themselves off from the stuff they feed upon. The harmful ramifications of not accepting self are endless, because one attitude leads to another.

He thinks well of others. This comes about automatically because of the one-ness of the self-other relationship. It is doubtful that there can be a self except in relation to others, and to accept one implies the acceptance of the other. The acceptance of others opens a whole world with which to relate. It is the opposite of the hostility which results from nonacceptance of self.

He therefore sees his stake in others. He sees that other people are the stuff out of which he is built. He has a selfish interest then in the quality of those around him and has responsibility in some degree for that quality. The whole matter of selfishness and altruism disappears when he realizes that self and other are interdependent—that we are indeed our brother's keeper, and he is ours. Coming into the awareness of mutual need modifies human behavior. He comes to see other people as opportunities, not for exploitation, but for the building of self. He becomes a loving person, so that he can get closer to the real source of his power.

He sees himself as part of a world in movement—in process of becoming. This follows from the whole notion of self and others and the acceptance that they can feed off each other and hence can improve. When one looks outward rather than inward, the idea of change—in self, in others, in things—becomes apparent. The acceptance of change as a universal phenomenon brings about modifications of personality. The person who accepts change and expects it behaves differently from the person who seeks to get everything organized so that it will be fixed from now on. He will not search for the firm foundation on which he can stand for the rest of his life. He will realize that the only thing he knows for sure about the future is that tomorrow will be different from today and that he can anticipate this difference with hopeful expectation.

Optimism is the natural outcome of an accepting view of self and hence of others. Such a person is a doer, a mobile person, one who relates himself in an active way with others. Such activity would be meaningless unless the person had hopes for improvement. As has been stated, today has no meaning except in relation to an expected tomorrow. This is the basis for hope, without which no one can thrive. Improvement is that which enhances and enriches self and others. Neither can be enhanced by itself.

The fully functioning personality, having accepted the ongoing nature of life and the dynamic of change, *sees the value of mistakes.* He knows he will be treading new paths at all times, and that, therefore, he cannot always be right. Rigid personalities suffer much from their need to be always right. The fully functioning personality will not only see that mistakes are inevitable in constantly breaking new ground, but will come to realize that these unprofitable paths show the way to better ones. Thus, a mistake, which no one would make if he could foresee it, can be profitable. In fact, much of what we know that is workable comes from trying that which is not. In our culture, it seems that most of our moral code is based on the values of rigid people who cannot bear to be wrong, and so, making a mistake is almost sinful. The effective person cannot afford to have his spirit of adventure thus hampered. He knows that the only way to find out is to go forward and to profit from experience—to make experience an asset.

The fully functioning self, seeing the importance of people, *develops and holds human values*. There is no one, of course, who does not come to hold values. Values come about through the life one lives, which determines what one comes to care about. The better the life, the better the values accumulated. The one who sees human beings as essential to his own enhancement develops values related to the welfare of people. Holding these values in a world which most people consider to be static, he encounters problems in meeting static mores. He is, therefore, on the creative edge of the generally accepted mores or morals. Values in terms of what is good for all people are continuously in conflict with materialistic values held by the majority.

He knows no other way to live except in keeping with his values. He has no need continuously to shift behavior, depending upon the kind of people nearest him. He has no need for subterfuge or deceit, because he is motivated by the value of facilitating self and others. While treading new paths is fraught with risk, he does not have to engage in a continuous guessing game to make his behavior match new people and also be consistent with what he has done before. A fully functioning person, holding human values, does not have to ask himself constantly what it was he said last week.

We are tempted to call this courage and integrity. This is another way of saying that one has what it takes to live as life really exists and to do it all in one piece. Can we call it courage when there is no alternative?

Since life is ever-moving and ever-becoming, *the fully functioning person is cast in a creative role*. But more than simply accepting this role, he sees creation going on all around him. He sees that creation is not something which occurred long ago and is finished, but that it is now going on and that he is part of it. He sees the evil of the static personality because it seeks to stop the process of creation to which we owe our world and our being. He exults in being a part of this great process and in having an opportunity to facilitate it. Life to him means discovery and adventure, flourishing because it is in tune with the universe.

Reference

Horney, K. (1945). *Our inner conflicts*. New York: W. W. Norton & Co.

Other Publications by the Author

Kelley, E. C. (1947). *Education for what is real*. New York: Harper & Brothers.
Kelley, E. C. (1951). *The workshop way of learning*. New York: Harper & Brothers.
Kelley, E. C., & Rasey, M. I. (1952). *Education and the nature of man*. New York: Harper & Brothers.

A Response to

"The Fully Functioning Self" by Earl C. Kelley

The Missing Context in "The Fully Functioning Self": Race and Class

Norman A. Newberg • *University of Pennsylvania, Philadelphia, Pennsylvania*

I n the summer of 1968, six years after the publication of *Perceiving, Behaving, Becoming,* I was attending a small invitational conference in Sausalito, California. The theme was the new educational programs coming out of "Third Force Psychology." The purpose of the conference—sponsored jointly by McGraw-Hill and Esalen Institute (the renowned Big Sur retreat center specializing in fostering human potential)—was to encourage young curriculum theorists and program developers to write books about an emerging field. Much of the talk focused on the perceived need for schools to tap human potential by promoting personal growth and self-actualization of students and teachers.

My colleague, Terry Borton, and I were co-directors of Philadelphia's Affective Education Program. We came to the conference fresh from race relations battles between the Philadelphia School District and representatives of the city's African American community and were deeply cognizant of how poverty (class) and race affected the school opportunities of inner-city students. Philadelphia, like other major cities, had been wracked by race riots in 1967. One of the battlegrounds was the School District of Philadelphia. The superintendent of schools, Mark Shedd, had asked me to mediate dialogue between alienated African Americans and school dis-

Note: References to Earl Kelley's 1962 chapter reflect the page numbers of the chapter as reprinted in this book (pp. 1–16).

trict personnel. In response to this request, I directed race relations retreats involving key school district administrators and African American parents and community organizers. Parents were angry and distrustful of the school district's seriousness in providing quality education to poor inner-city children that was academically rigorous and also responsive to the cultural differences of African American students. We were amazed that the conference participants did not seem to understand what was actually going on in urban schools. We, too, believed that schools could be more humane and sensitive to adults and children. However, unlike some of the emerging humanistic programs, our approach did not separate thinking from feeling. Rather, we worked to initiate a conversation between the domains, so that teachers could harness the power of each to promote the development of fully functioning students (Newberg and Loue, 1982).

In the Affective Education Program, for example, teachers learned how to express high expectations for student achievement; give students specific and timely feedback; develop an atmosphere of shared responsibility for teaching and learning; provide students with particular methods they can use to improve their attitude about learning; and build connections between academic content and students' personal lives. Teachers involved in the program learned to use techniques such as role playing, guided imagination experiences, simulations, and feedback at both personal and tasks levels. Teachers had also learned to involve students in establishing interpersonal rules and contracts for behavior as well as academic goals for achievement.

At the core of our approach was the belief that the context of our students' lives affected their capacity to achieve in school. In the United States, at that time, racism and poverty had clearly set arbitrary ceilings on the achievement of poor blacks and had limited their opportunities for jobs. Several researchers have found that if young black people believe that their future is predetermined by discriminatory practices of a dominant white society, they are less likely to accept schooling as the pathway to a successful life. After a history of limited access to social and economic resources through many generations, these students are more likely to resist school (Ogbu, 1982; Fordham, 1993). To protect their sense of self and their identity, they withdraw from school and "disidentify" (Steele, 1992). Then, as today, they put their trust in what they know. And, too often, what they know is reflected in the "code of the streets" (Anderson, 1994).

Earl Kelley's 1962 chapter, " The Fully Functioning Self," in *Perceiving, Behaving, Becoming: A New Focus for Education* focuses on using education to help a person make the most of one's self through nurturance rather than coercion or "tyranny." But, as at the Sausalito conference in the '60s, I was struck that the chapter makes no direct reference to problems of race or class. The illusion presented suggests that the self exists outside of history. How is this possible? Were the issues unimportant in the early '60s, when Kelley's chapter was published? Does the fact that Kelley did not focus on them make his thoughts less relevant today?

THE MISSING CONTEXT

Even though Kelley does not specifically mention racial discrimination as one of the "tyrants" that damage the self, certainly race was an issue in 1962, the year ASCD published *Perceiving, Behaving, Becoming*. Indeed, the previous decade set the stage for reframing attitudes about race. In 1954, the U.S. Supreme Court ruled in favor of Linda Brown, who had been kept out of a public elementary school in Topeka, Kansas. Basing his case largely on Kenneth Clark's research showing that black children formed negative self-images when raised in segregated environments, Thurgood Marshall argued successfully that "separate educational facilities are inherently unequal." And Chief Justice Warren, writing for the Court in the Brown case, concluded that separating children in schools on the basis of race alone "generates feelings of inferiority as to their status in the community that may affect their hearts and minds in a way unlikely ever to be undone." The ruling in favor of the plaintiff—combined with the Supreme Court's order in 1955 that federal courts act "to admit to public school on a racially nondiscriminatory basis with all deliberate speed the parties to these cases"—was a major victory for the Civil Rights movement. The ensuing struggle led to the passage of the Civil Rights Act of 1964. Clearly the courts had determined that segregated schools were injurious to the development of a healthy sense of self for U.S. children.

However, even in desegregated schools, blacks were mostly relegated to low ability tracks in the '60s, a new form of racism (Oakes, 1985). And the percentage of those blacks who graduated from high school and attended college was exceptionally low. In northern cities, blacks were not visible as high school teachers or as building principals, let alone district administrators. The courts alone could not change the context so that children disadvantaged by racism might succeed through education.

Then, as now, inner-city poverty was inextricably bound to issues of race (Nightingale, 1993). President Johnson conjoined race and poverty in his 1964 State of the Union address before Congress, when he declared a "War on Poverty." Johnson's declaration led to legislation that attempted to equalize resources and instruction so that poor students, which included large percentages of racial and ethnic minorities, could receive the same quality of education as their affluent fellows. The educational component of the "war" commenced in 1965 with the passage of the Elementary and Secondary Education Act (Title I).

In Kelley's chapter, the self appears to exist in a vacuum, largely a decontextualized abstraction. One wonders how Kelley can talk about a "fully functioning self" in schools that were inherently unequal and produced devastating "feelings of inferiority." Kelley, however, does assert that he abhors authoritarianism, concluding at one point that it seems likely "that very few survive home, church and school without damage to the self" (p. 13). He warns that it is relatively easy to recognize "grand scale" tyrants such as Hitler, while failing to recognize small tyrants that can "do more harm than grand ones. The small tyrant operates on the growing edge of the personality of the young" (p. 6). Ironically, he does not directly identify the corrosive forces of racism and poverty as tyrannical. They are not seen as obstacles that prevent the development of the fully functioning self; if they are seen, they are not discussed.

THE SELF IN CONTEXT

For Kelley, the fully functioning self has something to do with the core values a person holds, how a person sees himself or herself, and how that perception is always experienced in relation to others. Kelley posits an open, dynamic system of change and development within individuals and among them. The "self," for Kelley, is akin to "self-concept" and more than a little reminiscent of Erikson's theory of "identity" (1959, 1963). However, the contrast between Kelley and Erikson is instructive. While Kelley is ahistorical, Erikson sees the interconnectedness between identity formation and history. In a fascinating article that appeared in 1966 titled "The Concept of Identity in Race Relations," Erikson notes: "For identity development has its time, or rather two kinds of time: a *developmental stage* in the life of the individual, and a period of history. There is, then, also a complementarity of life-history and history" (p. 242). As a psychoanalyst, Erikson knew that he could not understand a patient without "taking a history." He was also keenly aware that one's personal story is related to the events that are being lived out in the history of one's time. Hence, in trying to understand major historical figures such as Gandhi, Luther, Jefferson, and Hitler, he was interested in how historical events shaped these political figures and how these leaders shaped history.

From Erikson we can identify some core problems with Kelley's approach. The self must function in context. Therefore, education must deal directly with the specific relation of self to context if it is to promote anyone's "fully functioning." Kelley's admonition that schools drop their tyranny and move more toward a process of mutual respect leading to cooperation between parents and children and teachers and students, while perhaps still applicable in 1962, was certainly not a new direction. What appeared to be new was the question of how education could be configured to help people in difficult, "tyrannical" contexts to become more fully functioning. This question was poignant at the time, and remains so today. The tyrannies of the jobless, violent, uncared for inner cities make education for contextual function ever more critical.

CHANGING THE CONTEXT

The "concentration effects" of poverty breed "social isolation" and thereby cut off "access to jobs, job networks, involvement in quality schools, and exposure to conventional role-models" (Wilson, 1987, pp. 58–59). Educational programs alone cannot ameliorate problems of this magnitude; these problems require a systemic approach. However, it is possible to make a positive difference in the lives of children trapped by poverty by addressing the problem from multiple perspectives.

What could Kelley's fully functioning self look like when race and poverty are an integral part of the context for change? What type of support would be needed to elevate youth beyond their circumstances? The following case example of a social, educational, and economic intervention illustrates the fact that the self (and its functioning) is influenced by the contexts it experiences. Since 1987, I have directed Say Yes to Education (SYTE), a tuition guarantee program, that serves 112 African American students from low-income families. The program promised these students, as they entered 7th grade, a fully paid-for two- or four-year college education or vocational training if they graduated from high school. Acting as a third-party intermediary between the school, the students, and their families, SYTE provided tutoring, counseling, SAT preparation, summer school enrichment, college visitations, advocacy at school, and job internships.

The program has maintained a 10-year relationship with these students, from junior high school through college. Although their school, home, and neighborhood environments were often chaotic and unreliable in terms of their support, SYTE tried to establish a relationship that offered "continuity of caring" (Noddings, 1992). Thus, the program attempted to change the context of school and the odds that overwhelm inner-city students. The program has made a critical assumption: that without transforming relationships and a widening sense of possibility, students cannot take advantage of better opportunities.

Kelley seems to concur with this point in the following excerpt from his chapter. He says that "to develop a fully functioning self, a person needs to have the opportunity to live the life good to live. This life, or his world, needs to be populated by people whom he can view as facilitating" (p. 11). He concludes this discussion with the following statement, which seems to romanticize poverty: "Facilitating people can be poor in material things. In fact, some of the happiest and most open people are found in poor material circumstances."

I fail to see how one can link happiness and openness with poverty. The social science literature of the past 40 years asserts that poverty limits opportunity, forces dependency, and relegates people to second-rate citizenship in terms of the services available, including the inferior quality of housing and education (Nightingale, 1993; Wilson, 1987). While it is true that some people who grow up in poverty succeed no matter how many obstacles they face, their life histories appear to be the exception and not the rule. Creating a fully functioning self requires sustained levels of support when other factors continually erode the resilience needed for youth to achieve their potential. This potential can be measured in real-life terms. SYTE students improved high school graduation rates by 100 percent when compared to a similar population. And of the 67 students who graduated from high school, 47 attended two- and four-year colleges (Schlesinger, 1993; Newberg and Sims, 1996).

With SYTE's sustained support through high school and college, many students have discovered new internal resources and, as a result, are developing more constructive self-concepts. Malleek (a pseudonym), now age 22, is a case in point. As a teenager, Malleek's sense of self was circumscribed by his violent surroundings. Finding a high school that could challenge him appropriately and channel his behavior so that he was socially responsible had been difficult. His behavior demonstrated that he disidentified with school and had aligned his future with life "in the streets." He was expelled from four schools before he finally graduated from high school. SYTE staff intervened repeatedly, counseling him to take responsibility for his behavior, and insisting that he return to school. Currently, he is a senior in a university majoring in business. Last semester he made the dean's list. In a recent interview, he reflected on how his sense of self had expanded because of a change in context. The university he was attending—and the sustained support SYTE offered—helped him make more life-affirming choices for himself:

> Sometimes I have to keep pinching myself that I'm up here in school [university]. When I was down in West Philly on that corner, you know, carrying the tool [gun] just not caring about nothing, you know? But now, I mean, all that's changed. When I go back down there now, it's like the blinders have been lifted off my eyes. I see other guys doing the stuff I used to do, and I can understand. Like damn, I was doing that! How could I have been so ignorant? So like, this college thing has showed me life could be a whole lot more and a lot of stuff that I was missing by being in that other type of life. Getting an education is not easy for me 'cause somebody expects you going against the grain when you doing it the right way, especially where I come from.

Malleek has analyzed his past circumstances and has decided that education will give him the capacity to live a more stable, meaningful life.

The cost of the SYTE intervention while students attended grade school was $1,200 per year for each student, plus the tuition guarantee for post-secondary schooling, which is funded by a philanthropic donor, George Weiss. The SYTE grade school expenditure, when combined with the per-pupil cost of the School District of Philadelphia, was still less than the average expenditure for a suburban school education.

What can we learn from the experiences of Malleek and other youth in the SYTE program? If inner-city children are to develop "fully functioning selves," they will need schools that sustain safe, caring environments and promote learning that is creative and rigorous. In these learning environments the basic unit should be a cohort of students and a team of teachers in which both parties maintain a continuous association for several years. Teachers and external partners need to make a commitment to the long-term social and academic development of children. In these schools, children's feelings of hopelessness, apathy, and opposition to education need to be addressed by caring educators knowledgeable in motivational strategies and capable of teaching to diverse learning styles. Teachers must appreciate that how children think about themselves as learners is connected to the context of their lives.

Elements of school organization like dividing large schools into "houses" and, more recently, charters and small learning communities, could provide the intimate teacher/student relationship that approximates some aspects of the SYTE intervention (Fine, 1994). Supportive services such as tutoring, counseling, mentoring, summer school, after-school programs, job internships, and college advising need to be part of the supportive mix to enable the growth toward a fully functioning person. Cities, states, and the federal government need to establish partnerships with the private sector to provide an umbrella of support for youth in financial need. Such assistance will enable public and private agencies to share in extending educational opportunities for youth, bringing the idea of a fully functioning person to increasing numbers of young people.

Kelley recognized that "endangering environments" breed isolation and limit the self's ability to mature. Poverty and racism are root causes of damaged and disabled selves and must be addressed before many of today's youth can find their pathway to a fully functioning self.

References

Anderson, E. (1994, March). The code of the streets. *Atlantic Monthly*, pp. 81–94.

Brown v. Board of Education, 347U.S.483 (1954).

Erikson, E. (1959). Identity and the life cycle. *Psychological Issues, 1*(1) (Monograph 1).

Erikson, E. (1963). *Childhood and society* (2nd ed.). New York: W. W. Norton and Co., Inc.

Erikson, E. (1966). The concept of identity in race relations: notes and queries. In T. Parsons and K. B. Clark (Eds.) (pp. 227–253). *The Negro American*. Boston: Houghton, Mifflin.

Fine, M. (Ed). (1994). *Chartering urban school reform*. New York: Teachers College Press.

Fordham, S. (1993). Those loud black girls: (black) women, silence, and gender "passing" in the academy. *Anthropology and Education Quarterly, 24*(10), 3–32.

Kelley, E. C. (1962). The fully functioning self. In A. W. Combs (Ed.), 1962 ASCD yearbook, *Perceiving, behaving, becoming: A new focus for education* (pp. 9–20). Alexandria, VA: Association for Supervision and Curriculum Development.

Newberg, N. (1995). Where inner-city students live versus how they learn. *University of Pennsylvania Law Review, 143*(5), 1415–1429.

Newberg, N., and Loue, W. (1982, May). Affective education addresses the basics. *Educational Leadership, 39*, 498–500.

Newberg, N., and Sims, R. (1996). Contexts that promote success for inner-city students. *Urban Education, 31*(2), 149–176.

Nightingale, C. H. (1993) *On the edge: A history of poor black children and their American dreams*. New York: Basic Books.

Noddings, N. (1992). *The challenge to care*. New York: Teachers College Press.

Oakes, J. (1985). *Keeping track*. New Haven, CT: Yale University Press.

Ogbu, J. (1982). Societal forces as a context of ghetto children's school failure. In L. Feagans and D. C. Farran (Eds.), *Language of children reared in poverty: Implications for evaluation and intervention*. New York: Academic Press.

P.L. 88-352, 78STAT.241 (1964, July 2). Vol. 78, p. 248, Statutes at Large.

Schlesinger, M. (1993). *A study of a tuition guarantee program*. Unpublished doctoral dissertation, Temple University, Philadelphia, Pennsylvania.

Steele, C. (1992, April). Race and the schooling of black Americans. *Atlantic Monthly*, pp. 68–78.

Wang, M. C., and Gordon, E. W. (Eds.). (1994). *Educational resilience in inner-city America: Challenges and prospects*. Hillsdale, NJ: Lawrence Erlbaum Associates, Inc.

Wilson, W. (1987). *The truly disadvantaged: The inner-city, the underclass, and public policy*. Chicago, IL: University of Chicago Press.

A Response to

"The Fully Functioning Self" by Earl C. Kelley

Educating Competent and Confident Individuals

Mary R. Sudzina • University of Dayton, Dayton, Ohio

arl Kelley takes on the home, church, and school as institutions that inhibited individuals' competence, self-esteem, and creativity in his 1962 treatise, "The Fully Functioning Self." Kelley believed that the self was achieved through social interaction with others, and by one's *perception* of his or her surroundings and capabilities. In the United States at that time, children were expected to fit into the existing culture and not to question adult authority. If individuals didn't fit in, they were punished or discriminated against. Children lived in an authoritarian world controlled by adults and subject to their rigid standards and scrutiny. As a result, they often believed themselves inadequate. Kelley concluded that adults and children alike appeared not to like themselves very much in this environment. Parents and teachers frequently used physical punishment and intimidation to coerce children into compliance, leaving very few individuals undamaged emotionally by their upbringing. "The evils of authoritarianism," Kelley warned in 1962, "are more extensive than is ordinarily understood" (p. 6).

Kelley and his colleagues clearly saw something lacking in the young people they were observing in the '50s and early '60s. Characteristics such as creativity, uniqueness, tolerance, compassion, diversity, self-esteem, altruism, and initiative, all seemed, in Kelley's view, to be drummed out of most students at an early age. Young people who escaped absorbing adults'

Note: References to Earl Kelley's 1962 chapter reflect the page numbers of the chapter as reprinted in this book (pp. 1–16).

negative authoritarian messages, and reached adulthood relatively unscathed, seemed few and far between. Adversarial relationships were often the result of power struggles between children and adults. Kelley urged parents and teachers to reach out and nurture children's individuality and uniqueness and to help children see themselves as adequate, rather than inadequate.

Kelley's admonitions have turned out to be more prophetic then he might have imagined. In the short span of a dozen years, young people of the '70s were questioning almost everything valued and overseen by the adults in the culture: government, politics, schooling, equal rights, religion, relationships, and parenting. The pendulum for young people had clearly swung from embracing adult values, standards, and ways of doing things, to formulating their own opinions, morality, and action plans.

EDUCATING THE FULLY FUNCTIONING SELF

To examine the relevance and implications of Kelley's ideas about teaching and learning for educators today, we will take stock of what it means to educate the "fully functioning self." First, we will glance back over the last several decades, then assess today's issues and concerns in school and society, and, finally, look ahead with an eye to the future: educating the whole child.

Looking Back

The '50s and early '60s were a time of relative stability and prosperity after World War II. They were also times when there was little tolerance or outlet for alternative ideas, clothes, opinions, and lifestyles. Sexual discrimination and racism, alluded to by Kelley, were yet to become broadbased issues in the schools and society. Although the Supreme Court declared in the 1954 *Brown v. the Board of Education of Topeka* decision that "separate but equal" schools for black children were unconstitutional, the country was not yet engaged in wide-scale school integration and busing. The American Dream for most citizens was to become part of a "melting pot" in which differences were glossed over in favor of homogeneity. Parents encouraged their children to be "American" and to lose their accents, ethnic traditions, and cultural identities in favor of Norman Rockwell-esque tableaus and holiday celebrations. It was important to fit in. New schools and mass housing developments, like Levittown, N.Y., abounded to accommodate the baby boomers, that bumper crop of children born after World War II. Although the Cold War was in full swing, all things seemed possible at home. Handsome and youthful John Kennedy and his stylish wife Jackie occupied the White House in 1960. The Youth Quake had begun. "Teenagers" and rock-and-roll music became inseparable cultural entities, much to the chagrin and consternation of many traditional parents.

I was a product of those times and public schools. In elementary school we took turns reading psalms from the Bible. We all recited "The Lord's Prayer" and then "The Pledge of Allegiance" with our hands over our hearts. Before my grammar school days were over, religion would be banned from the public schools. I remember teachers being firm but fair. We were expected to memorize the texts and to recite from our notes. Any student who couldn't learn the way the teacher taught, was, quite simply, treated as less intelligent. Parents saw education as key to a better life. Any disciplinary action taken at school would be reinforced at home. IQ, SAT, and achievement testing clearly seemed to favor certain groups over others. Fortunately, my testing was above average, and I was tracked into the higher-level classes. Even so, boys received the lion's share of teacher and parent attention and positive expectations—both in and out of the classroom.

Camelot ended the day Kennedy was shot. Our moral fiber was awakened by the Civil Rights Movement and the assassination of Martin Luther King Jr. The Vietnam War escalated and the draft loomed in our male classmates' future plans. We all knew someone who died in Vietnam. Many who could afford to go to college did so and delayed entering the service for four years. Many males enrolled in teacher training programs because teachers were exempt from the draft. The country was in turmoil. Vietnam polarized the United States, especially the youth, in ways few people could have imagined. Students protested and spoke out on their campuses, held rallies in Washington, D.C., and stormed their campus administrative buildings against a variety of issues.

To echo the anthem of Bob Dylan, king of the protest singers, "The times, they are a-changin'." I wonder if Kelley and his colleagues imagined that their concerns were soon to be amplified by wide-sweeping changes in the home, schools, and society. These changes were part of a larger series of societal changes brought about, in part, by the recent political and social upheavals. In addition, the sheer numbers of baby boomers moving through the system created a need for more and better schools, services, teachers, and parenting skills.

In the '70s, the schoolhouse door opened wider to accommodate those children who had been excluded or barred in the past. Children who were previously invisible from the public schools, those with handicaps and disabilities, were now guaranteed an appropriate and equal education. Schools became the domain of the underserved (poor, diverse, and handicapped) and became inclusive rather than exclusive institutions and communities of learning. Only now was the *Brown vs. the Board of Education* decision becoming a reality. Busing was frequently used to try to obtain racial balance and equality of educational opportunity for children in urban and suburban schools. In an attempt to meet everyone's needs, schools also expanded course curriculum options and electives.

The '70s were also the heyday of values clarification, parent counseling, sensitivity training, and psychological counseling in the schools, which tended to be Rogerian in nature. As a high school guidance counselor, I found myself confronted with a range of adolescent issues including drugs, alcohol, sex, homosexuality, abortion, disease, abuse, and suicidal depression. We were idealistic enough to believe that we could help our students, and their parents, in any situation if we were empathetic, helped them to understand what was happening, and explored alternatives. Wrong! Counseling, although helpful, was not a substitute or panacea for poor parenting, poor choices, or the inability to take positive or corrective action.

The '80s brought an infusion of learning styles, new math, and whole language to the curriculum. Again, schools were trying to be all things to all people. Government regulations abounded and many young people were discouraged from entering the teaching profession, as jobs were perceived to be scarce, the pay low, and the work demanding. Schools were just beginning to acknowledge and address the inequities in opportunities for men and women in schools for sports and higher-level math and science courses. The often liberal baby boomers of the '60s were now the teachers and parents of the children of the '80s. Issues were no longer as clear cut as they once appeared to be, and adults were struggling to find that happy medium between overcontrolling children and allowing them to take risks, fail, and succeed on their own. And it seemed as if *everyone*, whether in the profession or not, offered an opinion on what was wrong with the educational system.

This was also the time when the United States went from being a creditor nation to a debtor nation. Suddenly, the United States, which appeared to be winning the space race against the former Soviet Union, was in economic decline. Again, the schools were looked to for solutions as well as for blame in this new development.

Children and Schooling Today

The '90s have brought with them their own unique challenges. There has been a public outcry for "back to basics" in the curriculum, and a romanticized notion of the way reading, writing, and arithmetic were taught years ago as being so much better than they are today. That just isn't so. Students are so much more diverse today: intellectually, emotionally, sociologically, physically, ethnically, and culturally (Woolfolk, 1998). The demands on teachers and schools to provide the best education for each and every child would be a daunting task in the best of circumstances. Along with the multiple tracks in the curriculum to meet the needs of inclusive education, public schools now offer remedial and compensatory programs and tutors, as well as general, vocational, college preparatory, honors, advanced placement, and international baccalaureate programs. Teachers today are required to meet increased state and national certification standards for content area and professional preparation to deal with the wider range of student abilities, diversity, and needs in the schools (see, for example, NCATE Standards, 1978, 1995).

Previously, college-prep tracks and Scholastic Aptitude testing were the domain of the very brightest students, who (in their teachers' opinions) would benefit from such course work and go on to attend a four-year college. That, too, has changed. We now talk about multiple intelligences and "authentic" assessments, such as portfolios and projects, to supplement and complement teacher-made tests and standardized testing. More individuals are being encouraged to consider some form of higher education, and many more two- and four-year college programs now accommodate diverse student needs, ages, talents, and interests.

Another major change occurring in the classroom today is the shift from teacher-centered to student-centered classrooms. This shift is at the heart of *constructivism*, a learning paradigm in which the teacher is a *facilitator* of knowledge rather than the *source* of all that is to be known. Students today are seen as more capable of independent thought and action and can be willing partners in constructing shared meanings about course content, issues, and applications of knowledge. Seen in this light, learning is a process rather than a destination, and students are being given the tools and the opportunities to become lifelong learners.

Students today need yet another set of skills: technological competence and expertise in using computers and multimedia, and in accessing the Internet and World Wide Web. Schools and teachers, alike, are struggling to keep current with hardware and software. We face changes in teaching and learning communications, research, and resources from face-to-face exchanges, paper copies, hands-on texts, and hand-written assignments, to CU-SeeMe technology, voicemail, e-mail, and online video and audio, computer searches, texts, and assignments. Some of the obvious difficulties with these innovative approaches are the following:

- Getting such curriculum changes up and running requires an enormous amount of time, effort, and money.
- Revisions in the technology occur practically daily.
- Schools and children with few such resources available to them will be left behind.

Looking Ahead

The future will continue to be challenging, frustrating, and exciting for educators. The graduating classes in the year 2020 will be dramatically different from the youngsters Kelley and his colleagues observed. Not only will the schools be inclusive in meeting the needs of students with handicapping conditions, but predictions indicate that almost half of the population will be from African American, Asian, Hispanic, or other non-European ethnic groups (Grant & Sleeter, 1989). Sensitivity to cultural influences, and skills in cooperation and collaboration, will be key for teachers, parents, students, and the health of society.

Many educators today might long for those authoritarian days when schools were organized for the convenience of the teacher and were not responsive to the different learning needs of a wide range of children. The knowledge monopoly of the schools in the '50s and '60s has given way to competition with other sources of information and knowledge from television and video to computer and Internet access. Schools must attempt to stay current with this knowledge explosion as well as with the multiplicity and sources of information available.

I believe that at the heart of developing fully functioning young people are fully functioning adults as parents, educators, and spiritual leaders. They are some of the critical players (and offenders, in Kelley's view) in influencing students through their thoughts, words, and actions, about what it means to valued and encouraged to fulfill their potential and reach for their goals. But adults have needs, too. It takes many, many people to raise a "fully functioning" individual. Parents need support and respect, educators need to be appreciated and valued, and spiritual leaders' moral messages must be tempered with compassion as well as conviction. Children need to be nurtured and, at the same time, guided and disciplined fairly and democratically.

This difficult agenda should not discourage us from our calling as educators. Many of the ills that Kelley wrote about appeared to be a function of the adults' own socialization as youngsters in the lack of empathy, respect, and trust they received. Probably many of those well-intended adults were raising children in ways similar to their own upbringing. It is often difficult to unlearn the lessons of our own youth unless we are shown a better way and a reason to do so.

TO BE FULLY FUNCTIONING TODAY

The irony of Kelley's admonitions is that the very institutions that he and his colleagues were fearful of exerting too much control over youth 25 years ago are no longer those powerful forces today. The family, schools, and religion have lost significant influence in setting standards that positively shape students' character, behavior, values, and competence. Society and schooling have changed in ways that few could predict. Schools and teachers are assuming the roles that were previously the domain of parents and religion in providing guidelines and structure for young people.

Kelley and his colleagues were right to encourage adults to respect and positively support competence in young people. But they could not have predicted the sweeping sociological and political changes that would expand and challenge Kelley's idea of what it means to be "fully functioning."

Are Kelley's words still prophetic today? Do we still value and desire the "Fully Functioning Self"? Well, yes—and, no. Yes, in the sense that we want each child to be treated fairly and warmly, to receive appropriate academic preparation, and to be encouraged to believe in his or her capability to function successfully in society: intellectually, emotionally, and sociologically. No, if that means raising selfish individuals who feel good about themselves at the expense of others, who demonstrate learned helplessness instead of effort in mastering course content, and who lack the desire or skills to cooperate and get along with peers and adults. No, if it means having teachers who encourage only those children with whom they feel comfortable and who comply with their adult dictums. No, if we exclude children who have disabilities, live in poverty, come from single-parent homes, have apparent weaknesses, come from diverse backgrounds, or who are simply "different." Kelley's vision of what it means to be "fully functioning" has taken on new meanings.

To be "fully functioning" today, a person needs achievements in many areas. In addition to mastering school subjects and developing a positive perception of self, students today must be exposed to and become sensitive to the ethnic, physical, and cultural diversity of others. Today's students also need the ability to communicate, cooperate, and collaborate with others face-to-face and through information technology. All young people need a warm and supportive environment to grow and thrive, caring adults to serve as mentors and role models, and clear guidelines and expectations for academic performance, behavior, morality, and manners. No one person can do it all. Together we need to see ourselves as being connected to something greater than the sum of any one of our individual roles: the all-important task of raising the next generation of competent, confident, and compassionate human beings.

References

Grant, C., & Sleeter, C. (1989). Race, class, gender, exceptionality, and educational reform. In J. Banks & C. McGee Banks (Eds.), *Multicultural education: Issues and per-*

spectives (pp. 49–66). Boston: Allyn & Bacon.

Kelley, E. (1962). The fully functioning self. In A.W. Combs (Ed.), 1962 ASCD yearbook, *Perceiving, behaving, becoming: A new focus for education* (pp. 9–20). Alexandria, VA: Association for Supervision and Curriculum Development.

National Council for Accreditation of Teacher Education. (1978). *Certification standards for teacher preparation programs.* Washington, DC: NCATE.

National Council for Accreditation of Teacher Education. (1995). *Certification standards for teacher preparation programs* (Rev. ed.). Washington, DC: NCATE.

Woolfolk, A. (1998). The impact of culture and community. In *Educational psychology* (7th ed.) (pp. 160–201). Boston: Allyn & Bacon.

Toward Becoming a
Fully Functioning Person

Carl R. Rogers

This chapter originally appeared in the 1962 ASCD Yearbook, *Perceiving, Behaving, Becoming: A New Focus for Education*.

From the 1962 ASCD Yearbook

Toward Becoming a Fully Functioning Person

Carl R. Rogers • *University of Wisconsin*

I am sure that each of us has puzzled from time to time as to his own goals, and the goals which he believes would be desirable for others. "What is my purpose in life?" "What am I striving for?" "What do I want to be?" These are questions which every individual asks himself at one time or another, sometimes calmly and meditatively, sometimes in agonizing uncertainty or despair. They are old, old questions which have been asked and answered in every century of history. Yet they are also questions which every individual must ask and answer for himself, in his own way. They are questions which I, as a therapist, hear expressed in many differing ways as men and women in personal distress try to learn, or understand, or choose the directions which their lives are taking.

THE PROBLEM

As I have worked for many years with troubled individuals, I believe that I can discern a pattern, a trend, a direction, an orderliness, a commonality, in the tentative answers to these questions which these people have found for themselves. And so I would like to share with the reader the picture of the optimum human person, as I have formed this picture from my experience with my clients. It is my perception of what human beings appear to be striving for, when they feel free to choose their own direction. It is also my picture of what constitutes personal or psychological health.

The Background from Which the Problem Is Approached

I shall have to make it clear at the outset that my observations are made from a background of client-centered therapy. Quite possibly all successful psychotherapy has a similar personality outcome, but I am less sure of that than formerly, and hence wish it to be clear that I speak from a particular perspective. The trends I have observed have occurred in a relationship which, when it is at its best, partakes of these characteristics. The therapist has been willing to *be* his real feelings, has been willing to be genuine, in the relationship with the client. He has been able to enter into an intensely personal and subjective relationship with the client—relating not as a scientist to an object of study, not as a physician expecting to diagnose and cure, but as a person to a person.

The therapist feels this client to be a person of unconditional self-worth; of value no matter what his condition, his behavior, or his feelings. The therapist is able to let himself go in understanding this person; no inner barriers keep him from sensing what it feels like to be the client at each moment of the relationship, and he has been able to convey to the client something of this empathic understanding. It means that the therapist has been comfortable in entering this relationship fully, without knowing cognitively where it will lead, satisfied with providing a climate which will free the client to become himself.

For the client, this optimal therapy has meant an exploration of increasingly strange and unknown and dangerous feelings in himself; the exploration proving possible only because he is gradually realizing that he is accepted unconditionally. Thus, he becomes acquainted with elements of his experience which have in the past been denied to awareness as too threatening, too damaging to the structure of the self. He finds himself experiencing these feelings fully, completely, in the relationship, so that for the moment he *is* his fear, or his anger, or his tenderness, or his strength. And as he lives and accepts these widely varied feelings, in all their degrees of intensity, he discovers that he has experienced *himself*, that he *is* all these feelings. He finds his behavior changing in constructive fashion in accordance with his newly experienced and newly accepted self. He approaches the realization that he no longer needs to fear what experience may hold, but can welcome it freely as a part of his changing and developing self.

This is a thumbnail sketch of what client-centered therapy (Rogers, 1951) might be at its optimum. I give it here to suggest the kind of situation in which I have observed certain trends occurring in clients who have participated in such therapy. I would like now to proceed to my main concern: what are these directions, and what personality characteristics appear to develop in the client as a result of this kind of experience?

CHARACTERISTIC DIRECTIONS

What follows is based both upon clinical observation and upon research. It tries to present the trends I have seen in our clients, but it also pushes these trends to the limit, as it were, in order better to see the kind of person who would emerge if therapy were optimal, the kind of person who might be said to be the goal which individuals discover they are aiming toward.

An Increasing Openness to Experience

A major observation is that the individual moves toward being open to his experience. This is a phrase which has come to have increasingly definite meaning for me. It is the polar opposite of defensiveness. Defensiveness I have described in the past as being the organism's response to experiences which are perceived or anticipated as incongruent with the structure of the self. In order to maintain the self-structure, such experiences are given a distorted symbolization in awareness, which reduces the incongruity. Thus, the individual defends himself against any threat of alteration in the concept of self by not perceiving those meanings in his experience which contradict his present self-picture.

In the person who is open to his experience, however, every stimulus, whether originating within the organism or in the environment, would be freely relayed through the nervous system without being distorted by a defensive mechanism. There would be no need of the mechanism of "subception" (Lazarus & McCleary, 1951) whereby the organism is forewarned of any experience threatening to the self. On the contrary, whether the stimulus was the impact of a configuration of form, color, or sound in the environment on the sensory nerves, or a memory trace from the past, or a visceral sensation of fear or pleasure or disgust, the person would be "living it," would have it completely available to awareness.

Perhaps I can give this concept a more vivid meaning if I illustrate it from a recorded interview. A young professional man reports in the forty-eighth interview the way in which he has become more open to some of his bodily sensations, as well as other feelings.

> *Client:* It doesn't seem to me that it would be possible for anybody to relate all the changes that you feel. But I certainly have felt recently that I have more respect for, more objectivity toward, my physical make-up. I mean I don't expect too much of myself. This is how it works out: It feels to me that in the past I used to fight a certain tiredness that I felt after supper. Well now I feel pretty sure that I really am *tired*—that I am not making myself tired—that I am just physiologically lower. It seemed that I was just constantly criticizing my tiredness.
>
> *Therapist:* So you can let yourself *be* tired, instead of feeling along with it a kind of criticism of it.
>
> *Client:* Yes, that I shouldn't be tired or something. And it seems in a way to be pretty profound that I can just not fight this tiredness, and along with it goes a real feeling of *I've* got to slow down, too, so that being tired isn't such an awful thing. I think I can also kind of pick up a thread here of why I should be that way in the way my father is and the way he looks at some of these things. For instance, say that I was sick, and I would report this, and it would seem that overtly he would want to do something about it, but he would also communicate, "Oh, my gosh, more trouble." You know, something like that.
>
> *Therapist:* As though there were something quite annoying really about being physically ill.
>
> *Client:* Yeah, I am sure that my father has the same disrespect for his own physiology that I have had. Now last summer I twisted my back; I wrenched it; I heard it snap and everything. There was real pain there all the time at first, real sharp. And I had the doctor look at it and he said it wasn't serious; it should heal by itself as long as I didn't bend too much. Well this was months ago—and I have been noticing recently that—hell,

this is a real pain and it's still there—and it's not my fault, I mean it's—

Therapist: It doesn't prove something bad about you—

Client: No—and one of the reasons I seem to get more tired than I should maybe is because of this constant strain and so on. I have already made an appointment with one of the doctors at the hospital that he would look at it and take an X-ray or something. In a way I guess you could say that I am just more accurately sensitive—or objectively sensitive to this kind of thing. I can say with certainty that this has also spread to what I eat and how much I eat. And this is really a profound change, as I say, and of course my relationship with my wife and the two children is—well you just wouldn't recognize it if you could see me inside—as you have—I mean—there just doesn't seem to be anything more wonderful than really and genuinely—really *feeling* love for your own children and at the same time *receiving* it. I don't know how to put this. We have such an increased respect—both of us—for Judy, and we've noticed just—as we participated in this—we have noticed such a tremendous change in her—it seems to be a pretty deep kind of thing.

Therapist: It seems to me you are saying that you can listen more accurately to yourself. If your body says it's tired, you listen to it and believe it, instead of criticizing it, if it's in pain you can listen to that, if the feeling is really loving your wife or children, you can *feel* that, and it seems to show up in the differences in them, too.

Here, in a relatively minor but symbolically important excerpt, can be seen much of what I have been trying to say about openness to experience. Formerly he could not freely feel pain or illness, because being ill meant being unacceptable. Neither could he feel tenderness and love for his child, because such feelings meant being weak, and he had to maintain his facade of being strong. But now he can be genuinely open to the experience of his organism—he can be tired when he is tired, he can feel pain when his organism is in pain, he can freely experience the love he feels for his daughter, and he can also feel and express annoyance toward her, as he goes on to say in the next portion of the interview. He can fully live the experiences of his total organism, rather than shutting them out of awareness.

I have used this concept of availability to awareness to try to make clear what I mean by openness to experience. This might be misunderstood. I do not mean that this individual would be self-consciously aware of all that was going on within himself, like the centipede who became aware of all his legs. On the contrary, he would be free to live a feeling subjectively, as well as be aware of it. He might experience love, or pain, or fear, living in this attitude subjectively. Or he might abstract himself from this subjectivity and realize in awareness, "I am in pain"; "I am afraid"; "I do love." The crucial point is that there would be no barriers, no inhibitions, which would prevent the full experiencing of whatever was organismically present, and availability to awareness is a good measure of this absence of barriers.

Openness to experience is not a construct which is easy to measure with our present instruments, but such research as exists tends to support the notion that it is characteristic of those who are coping effectively with life. Chodorkoff (1954), for example, found in a very careful study that the better adjusted subjects perceived themselves more accurately. They were, that is, more open to the facts of their experience and thus perceived themselves in much the same way as they were seen by a group of competent and unbiased observers. Even more interestingly, they tended accurately to recognize threatening experiences (in this case tachistoscopically presented threatening words) more quickly than they recognized neutral experiences. They thus seemed very open even to stimuli which were threatening. The poorly adjusted group showed the reverse trend, and seemed to have a set toward keeping threatening experiences inadequately differentiated and inadequately symbolized.

Toward Becoming a Process

A second major trend which I have observed is that the individual moves toward more acceptantly being a process, a fluidity, a changing. He lives in a more existential fashion, living fully in each moment. Let me see if I can explain what I mean.

I believe it would be evident that for the person who was fully open to his experience, completely without defensiveness, each moment would be new. The complex configuration of inner and outer stimuli which exists in this moment has never existed before in just this fashion. Consequently, such a hypothetical person would realize that, "What I will be in the next moment, and what I will do, grow out of that moment, and cannot be predicted in advance either by me or by others." Not infrequently we find clients expressing this sort of feeling. Thus one, at the end of therapy, says in rather puzzled fashion, "I haven't finished the job of integrating and reorganizing myself, but that's only confusing, not discouraging, now that I realize this is a continuing process. . . . It is exciting, sometimes upsetting, but deeply encouraging to feel yourself in action and apparently knowing where you are going even though you don't always consciously know where that is."

One way of expressing the fluidity which is present in such existential living is to say that the self and personality emerge *from* experience, rather than experience being translated or twisted to fit a preconceived self-structure. It means that one becomes a participant in and an observer of the ongoing process of organismic experience, rather than being in control of it. As one client put it: "I have a feeling that what I have to do is to take more the position of passenger, rather than driver. See how things go when they're left alone. It's awful kind of scary—feeling that nobody's at the wheel. Of course it's a tremendously challenging feeling, too. Perhaps *this* is the key to freedom."

Or again, the same client, a bit later: "I'm not changing from *me* into something else, I'm changing from *me* to *me*. More like being an amoeba than a caterpillar-butterfly. The amoeba changes shape, but it's still an amoeba. In a way that's sort of a relief. I can keep the parts of me I really like. I don't have to chuck the whole thing, and start all over again."

Such living in the moment, then, means an absence of rigidity, of tight organization, of the imposition of structure on experience. It means instead a maximum of adaptability, a discovery of structure *in* experience, a flowing, changing organization of self and personality.

It is this tendency toward existential living which appears to me very evident in people who are involved in the process of psychological health. It means discovering the structure of experience in the process of living the experience. Most of us, on the other hand, bring a preformed structure and evaluation to our experience and never relinquish it, but cram and twist the experience to fit our preconceptions, annoyed at the fluid qualities which make it so unruly in fitting our carefully constructed pigeonholes. To open one's self to what is going on *now*, and to discover in that present process whatever structure it appears to have—this to me is one of the qualities of the healthy life, the mature life, as I see clients approach it.

An Increasing Trust in His Organism

Still another characteristic of the person who is living the process of health appears to be an increasing trust in his organism as a means of arriving at the most satisfying behavior in each existential situation. Again let me try to explain what I mean.

In choosing what course of action to take in any situation, many people rely upon guiding principles, upon a code of action laid down by some group or institution, upon the judgment of others (from wife and friends to Emily Post), or upon the way they behaved in some similar past situation. Yet as I observe the clients whose experiences in living have taught me so much, I find that increasingly such individuals are able to trust their total organismic reaction to a new situation because they discover to an ever-increasing degree that if they are open to their experience, doing what "feels right" proves to be a competent and trustworthy guide to behavior which is truly satisfying.

As I try to understand the reason for this, I find myself following this line of thought. The hypothetical person who is fully open to his experience would have access to all of the available data in the situation, on which to base his behavior; the social demands; his own complex and possibly conflicting needs; his memories of similar situations; his perception of the uniqueness of this situation. The data would be very complex indeed. But he could permit his total organism, his consciousness participating, to consider each stimulus, need, and demand, its relative intensity and importance, and out of this complex weighing and balancing, discover that course of action which would come closest to satisfying all his needs in the situation.

An analogy which might come close to a description would be to compare this person to a giant electronic computing machine. Since he is open to his experience, all of the data from his sense impressions, from his memory, from previous learning, from his visceral and internal states, are fed into the machine. The machine takes all of these multitudinous pulls and forces which are fed in as data, and quickly computes the course of action which would be the most economical vector of need satisfaction in this existential situation. This is the behavior of our hypothetical person.

The defects which in most of us make this process untrustworthy are the inclusion of information which does *not* belong to this present situation, or the exclusion of information which *does*. It is when memories and previous learnings are fed into the computations as if they were *this* reality, and not memories and learnings, that erroneous behavioral answers arise. Or when certain threatening experiences are inhibited from awareness, and hence are withheld from the computation or fed into it in distorted form, this too produces error. But our hypothetical person would find his organism thoroughly trustworthy, because all of the available data would be used, and it would be present in accurate rather than distorted form. Hence his behavior would come as close as possible to satisfying all his needs—for enhancement, for affiliation with others, and the like.

In this weighing, balancing, and computation, his organism would not by any means be infallible. It would always give the best possible answer for the available data, but sometimes data would be missing. Because of the element of openness to experience, however, any errors, any following of behavior which was not satisfying, would be quickly corrected. The computations, as it were, would always be in process of being corrected, because they would be continually checked against their consequences.

Perhaps the reader will not like my analogy of an electronic computing machine. Let me put it in more human terms. The client I previously quoted found himself expressing annoyance to his daughter, as well as affection, when he "felt like it." Yet he found himself doing it in a way which not only released the tension in himself, but which freed this small girl to voice her annoyances. He describes the differences between communicating his annoyance and directing his feeling of anger at, or imposing it on, her: " 'Cause it just doesn't feel like I'm imposing my feelings on her, and it seems to me I must show it on my face. Maybe she sees it as 'Yes, daddy is angry, but I don't have to cower.' Because she never *does* cower. This in itself is a topic for a novel, it just feels that good." In this instance, being open to his experience, he selects, with astonishing intuitive skill, a subtly guided course of behavior which meets his need for release of angry tension, but also satisfies his need to be a good father and his need to find satisfaction in his daughter's healthy development. Yet he achieves all this by simply doing the thing that feels right to him.

Another way of saying this is that the individual guides his behavior by the meanings which be discovers in the immediate feeling process which is going on within him. Gendlin (1961) terms this immediately present feeling process "experiencing," and shows how the individual can turn again and again to his experiencing to discover further meanings in it. The experiencing is thus a referent by which the individual may guide his behavior.

Observation has shown that clients who appear to have gained the most from therapy come to trust their experiencing. They accept the realization that the meanings implicit in their experiencing of a situation constitute the wisest and most satisfying indication of appropriate behavior. I think of one client who, toward the close of therapy, when puzzled about an issue, would put his head in his hands and say, "Now what *is* it I'm feeling? I want to get next to it. I want to learn what it is." Then he would wait, quietly and patiently, until he could discern the exact flavor of the feelings occurring in him. Often I sense that the client is trying to listen to himself, is trying to hear the messages and meanings which are being communicated by his own physiological reactions. No longer is he so fearful of what he may find. He comes to realize that his own inner reactions and experiences, the messages of his senses and his viscera, are friendly. He comes to want to be close to his inner sources of information rather than closing them off.

Again there is a bit of research evidence to indicate that this trust of one's own experiencing is associated with the healthy personality. Crutchfield (1955), in a most interesting study, presented potential military leaders with a situation in which the individual's clear perception and experience of a given situation appeared to be at variance with the judgment of all the other members of the group. Should he now rely on the evidence of his own senses or defer to the judgment of the group? The evidence shows that those who trusted their own experiencing were better adjusted individuals, more mature, with greater leadership ability. Those who distrusted their own sensing of the situation and adopted the group judgment were the less mature, less well adjusted persons.

It seems to be this trust of his own experiencing which guided the scientific behavior of Einstein, holding him toward a given direction, long before be could give any completely conscious and rational basis for it.

During this initial period he simply trusted his total organismic reaction. He says, "During all those years there was a feeling of direction, of going straight toward something concrete. It is, of course, very hard to express that feeling in words, but it was decidedly the case, and clearly to be distinguished from later considerations about the rational form of the solution" (Wertheimer, 1945, pp. 183–184). This is the type of behavior which is also, I believe, characteristic of the person who has gained greatly from therapy.

SOME IMPLICATIONS

The three trends I have tried to describe—toward openness to experience, living as a process, and trust of one's own experiencing—add up to the fact that the person in whom they are observed is becoming a more fully functioning person. This picture of a more fully functioning individual has many implications, but I will restrict myself to pointing out three which I believe have special importance.

Integration Is Implied

The trends I have presented describe an individual who is becoming integrated. He is unified within himself from the surface level to the level of depth. He is becoming "all of one piece." The distinctions between "role self" and "real self," between defensive facade and real feelings, between conscious and unconscious, are all growing less the further these trends continue. All that the individual experiences and is, within the envelope of his organism, is increasingly available to his conscious self, to himself as a person. There is a continuing growth of good communication between all the different aspects and facets of himself.

Creativity Is Implied

Watching my clients, I have come to a much better understanding of creative people. El Greco, for example, must have realized, as he looked at some of his early work, that "good artists do not paint like that." But somehow he trusted sufficiently his own experiencing of life, the process of himself, so that he could go on expressing his own unique perceptions. It was as though he could say, "Good artists do not paint like this, but *I* paint like this." Or, to move to another field, Ernest Hemingway was surely aware that "good writers do not write like this." But fortunately he moved toward being Hemingway, being himself, rather than toward someone else's conception of a good writer.

Einstein seems to have been unusually oblivious to the fact that good physicists did not think his kind of thoughts. Rather than drawing back because of his inadequate academic preparation in physics, he simply moved toward being Einstein, toward thinking his own thoughts, toward being as truly and deeply himself as he could. This is not a phenomenon which occurs only in the artist or the genius. Time and again in my clients, I have seen simple people become significant and creative in their own spheres, as they have developed more trust of the processes going on within themselves, and have dared to feel their own feelings, live by values which they discover within, and express themselves in their own unique ways.

Such a person would, I believe, be recognized by the student of evolution as the type most likely to adapt and survive under changing environmental conditions. He would be able creatively to make sound adjustments to new as well as old conditions. He would be a fit vanguard of human evolution.

Trustworthiness of Human Nature Is Implied

It will have been evident that one implication of the view presented here is that the basic nature of the human being, when functioning freely, is constructive and trustworthy. For me this is an inescapable conclusion from a quarter century of experience in psychotherapy. When we are able to free the individual from defensiveness, so that he is open to the wide range of his own needs, as well as to the wide range of environmental and social demands, his reactions may be trusted to be positive, forward-moving, constructive. We do not need to ask who will socialize him, for one of his own deepest needs is for affiliation and communication with others. When he is fully himself, he cannot help but be realistically socialized. We do not need to ask who will control his aggressive impulses, for when he is open to all of his impulses, his need to be liked by others and his tendency to give affection are as strong as his impulses to strike out or to seize for himself. He will be aggressive in situations in which aggression is realistically appropriate, but there will be no runaway need for aggression. His total behavior, in these and other areas, when he is open to all his experience, is balanced and realistic—behavior which is appropriate to the survival and enhancement of a highly social animal.

I have little sympathy with the rather prevalent concept that man is basically irrational, and that his impulses, if not controlled, would lead to destruction of others and self. Man's behavior is exquisitely rational, moving with subtle and ordered complexity toward the goals his organism is endeavoring to achieve. The tragedy for most of us is that our defenses keep us from being aware of this rationality, so that consciously we are moving in one direction, while organismically we are moving in another. But in our hypothetical person there would be no such barriers, and he would be a participant in the rationality of his organism. The only control of impulses which would exist or which would prove necessary is the natural and internal balancing of one need against another and the discovery of behaviors which follow the vector most closely approximating the satisfaction of all needs. The experience of extreme satisfaction of one need (for aggression, sex, etc.) in such a way as to do violence to the satisfaction of other needs (for companionship, tender relationship, etc.)—an experience very common in the defensively organized person—would simply be unknown in our hypothetical individual. He would participate in the vastly complex self-regulatory activities of his organism—the psychological as well as physiological thermostatic controls—in such a fashion as to live harmoniously, with himself and with others.

BECOMING A FULLY FUNCTIONING PERSON

Let me conclude by drawing together these observational threads into a more unified strand. As I have observed individuals who appear to have made important strides toward psychological health, I believe they may be thought of as moving toward an implicit goal—that of becoming a fully functioning person.

I find such a person to be a human being in flow, in process, rather than having achieved some state. Fluid change is central in the picture.

I find such a person to be sensitively open to all of his experience—sensitive to what is going on in his environment, sensitive to other individuals with whom he is in relationship, and sensitive perhaps most of all to the feelings, reactions, and emergent meanings which he discovers in himself. The fear of some aspects of his own experience continues to diminish, so that more and more of his life is available to him.

Such a person experiences in the present, with immediacy. He is able to live in his feelings and reactions of the moment. He is not bound by the structure of his past learnings, but these are a present resource for him, insofar as they relate to the experience of the moment. He lives freely, subjectively, in an existential confrontation of this moment of life.

Such a person is trustingly able to permit his total organism to function freely in all its complexity in selecting, from the multitude of possibilities, that behavior which in this moment of time will be most generally and genuinely satisfying. He thus is making use of all of the data his nervous system can supply, using this data in awareness, but recognizing that his total organism may be, and often is, wiser than his awareness.

Such a person is a creative person. With his sensitive openness to his world, and his trust of his own ability to form new relationships with his environment, he is the type of person from whom creative products and creative living emerge.

Finally, such a person lives a life which involves a wider range, a greater richness, than the constricted living in which most of us find ourselves. It seems to me that clients who have moved significantly in therapy live more intimately with their feelings of pain, but also more vividly with their feelings of ecstasy; that anger is more clearly felt, but so also is love; that fear is an experience they know more deeply, but so is courage; and the reason they can thus live fully in a wider range is that they have this underlying confidence in themselves as trustworthy instruments for encountering life.

I believe it will have become evident why, for me, adjectives such as happy, contented, enjoyable, do not seem quite appropriate to any general description of this process I have called psychological health, even though the person in this process would experience each one of these feelings at appropriate times. But the adjectives which seem more generally fitting are adjectives such as enriching, exciting, rewarding, challenging, meaningful. This process of healthy living is not, I am convinced, a life for the fainthearted. It involves the stretching and growing of becoming more and more of one's potentialities. It involves the courage to be. It means launching oneself fully into the stream of life. Yet the deeply exciting thing about human beings is that when the individual is inwardly free, he chooses this process of becoming.

Selected References

Chodorkoff, B. (1954). Self-perception, perceptual defense, and adjustment. *Journal of Abnormal and Social Psychology, 49*, 508–512.

Crutchfield, R. S. (1955). Conformity and character. *American Psychologist, 10*, 191–198.

Gendlin, E. (1961). Experiencing: A variable in the process of therapeutic change. *American Journal of Psychotherapy, 15*, 233–245.

Lazarus, R. S., & McCleary, R. A. (1951). Autonomic discrimination without awareness: A study of subception. *Psychological Review, 58*, 113–122.

Rogers, C. R. (1951). *Client-centered therapy: Its current practice, implications, and theory.* Boston: Houghton Mifflin Co.

Wertheimer, M. (1945). *Productive thinking.* New York: Harper & Brothers.

Other Publications by the Author

Rogers, C. R. (1951). *Client-centered therapy: Its current practice, implications, and theory.* Boston: Houghton Mifflin Co.

Rogers, C. R. (1961). *On becoming a person.* Boston: Houghton Mifflin Co.

A Response to
_____

"Toward Becoming a Fully Functioning Person"
by Carl R. Rogers

Carl Rogers: His Enduring Message

H. Jerome Freiberg, University of Houston, Houston, Texas

In "Toward Becoming a Fully Functioning Person," Carl Rogers asks three universal questions, "What is the purpose of my life?" "What am I striving for?" "What do I want to be?" They form the basis of his focus on human learning: that the source of problems and their solutions rest with the individual. These questions could form the foundations to learning. Students as well as teachers might reflect upon them each day.

Rogers also presents three trends he has observed in his years as a therapist. First, healthy individuals are open to experience: they don't hide from life, they explore it. Second, living is a process: openness to experience necessitates an absence of rigidity and allowing the time needed to change. Third, people must trust their own experiences. Rogers notes Albert Einstein's trust in his own experience, which guided his scientific behavior, "holding him toward a given direction, long before he could give any completely conscious and rational basis for it." As Einstein explained:

> During all those years there was a feeling of direction, of going straight toward something concrete. It is, of course, very hard to express that feeling in words, but it was decidedly the case, and clearly to be distinguished from the later considerations about the rational form of the solution. (Wertheimer [as cited in Rogers, p. 47]).

_____
Note: References to Carl Rogers' 1962 chapter reflect the page numbers of the chapter as reprinted in this book (pp. 35–51).

FACILITATION: CREATING A BALANCE

While few reviewers have the opportunity to ask questions directly to their authors, I had the rare opportunity to spend a day with Carl Rogers. In January 1984, I met Carl at his home in La Jolla, California. Our meeting took the form of a free flowing discussion of educational issues and ideas. The conversations were recorded, and excerpts from those discussions are included here.[1]

We met in the garden of his home on a sunny and pleasant January morning surrounded by roses and other flowers, which Carl tended himself. His 1950s home, a simple one-story open design near the top of a hill overlooking the Pacific Ocean, was heated by solar power. His homestead, however, was overshadowed by multi-story, million-dollar homes with signs warning that armed guards protected the properties. There was no such sign in front of Carl's home.

At 81, Carl Rogers, widowed after 55 of marriage, had few illusions about the challenges of life, but he also had a remarkably positive view about life that had sustained him through difficult times. I shared a story with him that was told to me by a colleague:

> Someone stopped Carl Rogers on the street in San Diego and asked him where the Hyatt Regency Hotel was. Rogers stopped, thought for a moment, and asked the man, "Where would you like it to be?"

Rogers roared with laughter, adding that there are many common misconceptions about his work. Being facilitative, he emphasized, does not mean being disengaged or directionless.

His path to creating a new direction for psychotherapy was during a time when the behavioral theories of Watson, Pavlov, and others of his time ruled. His first clinical position was in Rochester, New York, where many of his clients were "delinquent and underprivileged children sent to us by the courts and agencies" (Kirshenbaum & Henderson, 1989, p. 11). It was here that Carl realized that he could solve a problem for the client but the client would return with a new problem. He soon discovered that

---

[1]Two years before, I had assisted Carl on his revision of the second edition of *Freedom to Learn* (1982). Then, after Carl's death in 1987, with the support of his daughter, Natalie Rogers, and the publisher, I revised *Freedom to Learn* into its third edition (1994).

helping the individual solve his or her own problems and facilitating growth, not dissecting a life, was a more meaningful direction. He believed the facilitator is not a remote disengaged partner. "We must also use our own experience and expertise," he said, "to wisely question, interpret, inform, reinforce, or otherwise help lead our charges in positive growthful directions" (Kirshenbaum & Henderson, 1989 p. xv). Facilitation is a delicate balance between guidance and control, one that is built carefully over time. The vignette in "Toward Becoming a Fully Functioning Person" in which Rogers listens to a client talk about his increasing openness to experiences shows how this facilitation works in a one-to-one setting (pp. 42–43).

A POSITIVE ENVIRONMENT FOR GROWTH

Rogers also felt that maintaining healthy environments requires ongoing attention and guidance. I had asked Rogers how to maintain a positive environment for children and youth. Rogers shared this understanding during our conversations:

> I work every day in my garden. The roses, flowers, and plants do well in southern California climate if you water, provide natural food, and till the soil to allow oxygen to reach the roots. I am aware that weeds are always present. It is the constant caring that prevents the weeds from taking over the garden. Person-centered education is much like my rose garden—it needs a caring environment to sustain its beauty. (Rogers, 1984)

Long before *The 7 Habits of Highly Effective People*, *Chicken Soup for the Soul*, and *Multiple Intelligences*, Carl Rogers talked about basic principles of human interaction: Congruence, Unconditional Positive Regard, and Empathic Understanding and the need for Reflection and Awareness. When *Congruence* is present, learning is made real to the learner, and the facilitators of learning are real people without pretense or facade. *Unconditional Positive Regard*, a basic principle for human interaction, should be a given for learners in the classroom that is without preconditions. Also needed are *Empathic Understanding*—the ability to see the world through the eyes of the learner—and *Reflection*, the ability of the facilitator to contemplate the conditions at hand and respond appropriately in the best interest of the learner and the teacher. *Awareness* is the ability of the learner to seek out congruence, acceptance, empathy, and reflection in the learning environment. It is not enough for the conditions to exist; learners must have the conditions communicated to them, and they must understand them (Rogers & Freiberg, 1994).

THE PRINCIPLES OF FREEDOM AND LEARNING

In our meeting in 1984, Carl and I spent part of our time together discussing the issues of freedom, responsibility, and the importance of learning from mistakes. I had asked him specifically about the issues of *freedom* and control. Rogers responded by stating:

> Granting freedom is not a method, it's a philosophy and, unless you really believe that students can be trusted with responsibility, you won't be successful. Now, you can't build that philosophy out of thin air; you have to build it out of experience . . .
> . . . [Freedom] is built on experience, and that is achieved by taking it in small steps that you can really stand by. . . . Don't grab freedom if you are uneasy about it, better to [have] a little freedom that you can be easy with, than to try to go all the way in giving your students responsibility for their learning and then getting cold feet and trying to pull it back to yourself. That can be disastrous. It's better to take small steps . . . that you really mean and can stand by than to take it [freedom] all at once. . . . Giving students freedom means that they are going to make some mistakes in the handling of that responsibility. And that means a complete rethinking of the ordinary classroom procedure . . . mistakes are the most valuable way of learning provided the students are encouraged to examine what they did. (Rogers, 1984)

Rogers and the other authors of *Perceiving, Behaving, Becoming* were not about prescriptions—they set basic principles and asked us to set our lives against these principles. It is perhaps up to others to make the translation from theories to practice.

Theories need time to be tested. Some of Albert Einstein's theories were only affirmed 50 or more years later with space exploration and the development of computer technology. Psychological theories also require time to prove. Unlike most mathematical ones, many social theories may be partially proven. The field of humanistic psychology—with the work of Rogers, Combs, and Maslow as its leading proponents—has not been researched extensively in public schools. What has been tested is providing pieces to the puzzle. It has been left to others (Aspy & Roebuck, 1977; Schaps & Solomon, 1990; Lewis, Schaps, & Watson, 1996) to demonstrate that caring environments that respect the learner by displaying Empathy, Congruence, and Unconditional Positive Regard have provided important supports for the learner, measurable in ways that are understandable to the public. Increased achievement, better attendance, and healthier school climates are outcomes that have real meaning.

FROM TRUST COMES SELF-DISCIPLINE

When I ask teachers to identify the attributes of the best teachers they have ever had, they highlight affective rather than cognitive qualities on almost a three-to-one basis. Caring, empathy, friendliness, and good listener head the list.

In my own work, I have attempted to realize the necessary conditions for change in classroom and school climate by applying Carl's principles to personal relationships between teacher and student and among students. I have found that the more you control children, the more you need to control them. The emphasis on compliance rather than self-discipline leads to dissatisfied teachers and learners. A program has evolved from my research and work with classrooms and schools in inner cities called Consistency Management & Cooperative Discipline (CMCD [see Freiberg, 1996, and Freiberg, 1999, for a description]). The research findings over the last decade suggest that students can move from being *tourists* to *citizens* in their learning and participation in the workings of their educational environments (Freiberg, Prokosch, Treister, & Stein, 1990; Freiberg, Stein, & Huang, 1995; Opuni, 1997). The positive outcomes of CMCD include improvements in teacher and student attendance, school and classroom climate, and student discipline; significant gains in student learning as measured by standardized national tests; increased time for teachers to teach; and dramatic reductions in school violence. It is clear that, given the knowledge and organizational opportunities, teachers will begin to create a positive climate for students. Students, in turn, will become citizens of their learning environments. They will support their teachers by forming partnerships of knowledge rather than becoming adversarial combatants.

Rogers emphasized the need for trust. A teacher at an inner-city middle school where the CMCD program was developing shared the journals of students who managed the classroom themselves when their teacher was absent and the substitute did not show. The students took attendance and sent it to the office, wrote in their journals, and completed their school work. Sergio, an 8th grader, describes that day:

> I feel lucky today because the day has just started, and we have already been trusted in something we have never been trusted on, being alone. It is 8:15 and everything is cool. Nothing is even wrong.

Students learn self-discipline through experience. Sergio's teacher had shared the responsibilities of the classroom, and the students experienced freedom along with responsibility. They knew what to do without adult supervision—and when the opportunity arose they were prepared to respond in a meaningful way.

IS ROGERS' MESSAGE STILL RELEVANT?

Does Rogers have a message for the teachers of today and tomorrow? I would think a very important message. After classroom management, the next greatest concern of teachers and parents is student motivation, the negative side of which is exhibited through apathy, drug abuse, and suicide. These growing problems are symptoms of an even greater problem: the lack of freedom for human interaction.

Learning in most schools is a lonely, solitary experience. Students must sit quietly and listen to others speak without the opportunity for meaningful interaction. We expect school to act as socializer for society, yet we seldom encourage dialogue and interchange among students. We assume higher-level and critical thinking skills will emerge from academic rigor and are mystified when our students are unable to make decisions for themselves.

Schools and classrooms occupy more than 50 percent of a child's waking day, and there is a need for *real change*. We should not confuse mere activities for a metamorphosis from the status quo. Change results in a different feel, look, and way of thinking and interacting with others. The sharing of time in the classroom with students, providing the opportunity for students to learn from one another, and creating a level of shared decision making and choice are necessary if students are to become fully functioning individuals.

Few would disagree that we need to create classrooms that are democratic and caring. How we arrive at this destination has been a source of debate for decades. Providing freedom and choice in the classroom is a necessity if we are to keep the world free and prosperous. A democracy depends on an informed, educated, and involved electorate. That involvement begins with four-year-olds and carries forward throughout the child's life into adulthood.

Rogers and other humanists have been criticized for being "romantics" and not in tune with the harsh realities of life. In my time with Carl, I found him to be very much in tune with reality; he just was not willing to accept conditions in which children were viewed as lesser persons.

References

Aspy, D., & Roebuck, F. (1977). *Kids don't learn from people they don't like*. Amherst, MA: Human Resource Development Press.

Freiberg, H. J. (1994). Understanding resilience: Implications for inner-city schools and their near and far communities. In M.C. Wang and E.W. Gordon (Eds.), *Educational resilience in inner-city America: Challenges and prospects*. Hillsdale, NJ: Lawrence Erlbaum.

Freiberg, H. J. (1996). From tourists to citizens in the classroom. *Educational Leadership*, 54(1), 32–36.

Freiberg, H. J. (Ed.). (1999). *Beyond behaviorism: Changing the classroom management paradigm*. Needham Heights: Allyn & Bacon.

Freiberg, H. J., Prokosch, N., Treister, E. S., & Stein, T. A. (1990). Turning around five at-risk elementary schools. *Journal of School Effectiveness and School Improvement*, 1(1), 5–25.

Freiberg, H. J., Stein, T., & Huang, S. (1995). The effects of classroom management intervention on student achievement in inner-city elementary schools. *Educational Research and Evaluation*, 1(1), 33–66.

Kirshenbaum, H., & Henderson, V. (1989). (Eds.). *The Carl Rogers reader*. Houghton Mifflin: Boston.

Lewis, C. C., Schaps, E., & Watson, M. S. (1996). The caring classroom's academic edge." *Educational Leadership, 54*(1), 15–21.

Olatokunbo, S. F., & Slavin, R. E. (1998). Schoolwide reform models: What works? *Phi Delta Kappan, 79*(5), 370–379.

Opuni, K. A. (1997). *Project GRAD evaluation report.* Houston Independent School District, Houston, Texas.

Rogers, C. R. (1962). Toward becoming a fully functioning person. In A. W. Combs (Ed.), 1962 ASCD yearbook, *Perceiving, behaving, becoming: A new focus for education* (pp. 21–33). Alexandria, VA: Association for Supervision and Curriculum Development.

Rogers, C. R. (1982). *Freedom to learn.* (2nd ed.). Columbus, OH: Merrill.

Rogers, C. R. (1984). Personal communication with H. J. Freiberg.

Rogers, C. R., & Freiberg, H. J. (1994). *Freedom to learn.* (3rd ed.). Columbus: Merrill.

Schaps, E., & Solomon, D. (1990). Schools and classrooms as caring communities. *Educational Leadership, 48*(3), 38–42.

A Response to

"Toward Becoming a Fully Functioning Person"
by Carl R. Rogers

Austin High School for Teaching Professions and the "Fully Functioning Person"

Dottie Bonner • Austin High School for Teaching Professions, Houston, Texas

Carl Rogers said that one "characteristic of the person who is living the process of health appears to be an increasing trust in his organism as a means of arriving at the most satisfying behavior in each existential situation" (p. 44). Rogers' ideas are alive and well at Austin High School for Teaching Professions (AHSTP), a magnet school in Houston, Texas. Since its opening in 1982, its faculty and students, who have also expressed a desire to become teachers, have embraced Rogers' concepts.

Psychologically healthy people, said Rogers, "are able to trust their total organismic reaction to a new situation because they discover to an ever-increasing degree that if they are open to their experience, doing what 'feels right' proves to be a competent and trustworthy guide to behavior which is truly satisfying" (p. 44). The person-centered curriculum at AHSTP provides high school students with new situations where they are encouraged to respond by doing what "feels right." Students have an opportunity to visit the state capitol and voice their opinions about educational issues. In their issues class, students choose a topic, pick a side, select their opponents, and then conduct a debate for their final exam. Seniors experience teaching as interns four days a week.

Note: References to Carl Rogers' 1962 chapter reflect the page numbers of the chapter as reprinted in this book (pp. 35–51).

LIVING IN THE MOMENT

The sophomores at AHSTP are Big Brothers and Big Sisters for 5th grade students at a local elementary school. We emphasize intergenerational support of high school students with younger learners, creating a caring environment for interaction. Although these are visits with planned activities, the primary objective is for the high school students to be able to spend a prolonged period of time with a younger student. Sometimes their little brothers or sisters may just want to talk. At other times the high school students might help the 5th graders with their lessons. Occasionally, plans may not go as they had expected. We trust the high school students to do the right thing at the moment it needs to be done. What we want them to learn is to go with the flow of what's happening in the lives of students.

Rogers said,

> Such living in the moment, then, means an absence of rigidity, of tight organization, of the imposition of structure on experience. It means instead a maximum of adaptability, a discovery of structure *in* experience, a flowing, changing organization of self and personality. (p. 43)

The program, which was added to the AHSTP curriculum in 1991, has been tremendously successful. At the end of the first year, 5th grade teacher Sarah Green reported, "My students' grades went up, discipline problems decreased, and attendance improved. On the days when the high school students were to be at the elementary school, I usually had 100 percent attendance." We have seen these same kinds of results every year.

Green teaches a bilingual class. One of her students, Maria, (a pseudonym), had been in the United States only a year and a half and spoke very little English. Unfortunately, her big sister didn't speak Spanish. The Big Sister would draw pictures or diagrams as she worked with Maria, and she made flash cards at home to use during their sessions. Maria made tremendous improvement during the year. She took the Big Brother/Sister program so seriously," said Green,

> Maria's self-confidence increased as rapidly as did her English. She applied for and was admitted to a program for gifted and talented students the next year. She's still there and making excellent grades.

"I really enjoyed the program," Maria said, "because it helped me really understand the need to understand English." At that particular moment, Maria saw the need to improve her English. She and her big sister were *living in the moment, experiencing a maximum of adaptability, discovering structure in experience*, and Maria was reorganizing herself and her personality. Maria realized that there were myriad exciting and challenging educational opportunities out there, and that she would not be able to fully access these opportunities unless she were as fluent in English as she was in Spanish.

BECOMING FULLY FUNCTIONING PERSONS

Year after year, the high school students have unanimously reported how much they enjoyed being Big Brothers and Sisters. Recently, a bus load of students returned from a four-day trip taken with their little brothers and sisters to one of the school district's outdoor education centers. The high school students had assisted the camp personnel as the 5th graders rode horses, paddled canoes, tested water samples, and told stories around campfires. As they poured off the bus, I was inundated with enthusiastic screams: "It was fantastic!" "Great!" "We had so much fun!" "Those kids are so neat!" "My student was afraid of the horses, so I had to go first!" "We went hiking every day! If it rained, we put on yellow slickers and just kept on going!"

Recently, the 5th graders visited the high school. Entering the classroom, I found the room filled with students, large and small. In groups of two, three, or four they were huddled together with copies of the Austin High School Course Catalog. The younger students were pointing, asking questions, smiling, and listening intently to the high school students. I don't think anyone responsible for developing the course catalog could ever have dreamed about the amount of excitement it would be creating. I certainly hadn't. Something so basic, but the elementary students were getting a glimpse into life in high school and enjoying the attention of the older students.

The high school students were the experts, full of information and expertise on the nuances of high school life. I believe that if any "expert" had seen that classroom at that moment, he or she would have immediately advocated cross-age instruction as a strategy to increase students' active involvement in their own learning. Before they returned to their own school, the 5th graders toured the school and had lunch in the cafeteria with their Big Brothers and Sisters.

As I watched the faces of my students and of the 5th graders, I was reminded of the adjectives Rogers used to describe the lives of fully functioning persons: enriching, exciting, rewarding, challenging, and meaningful. I thought how well they described the moment and our attempts to assist our students on their way to becoming fully functioning persons.

A Response to

"Toward Becoming a Fully Functioning Person"
by Carl R. Rogers

Quest High School's Mission and the "Fully Functioning Person"

Lawrence Kohn • Quest High School, Humble, Texas

"When we are able to free the individual from his defensiveness," said Carl Rogers, "so that he is open to the wider range of his own needs, as well as to the wide range of environmental and social demands, his reactions may be trusted to be positive, forward-moving, constructive" (p. 48). This implication is highly relevant in today's secondary classrooms. It is achieved by creating a person-centered environment in which students feel ownership in the school and a trusting relationship with their teachers. This person-centered environment supported by Carl Rogers is practiced in the high school where I facilitate learning, Quest High School in Humble, Texas.

Quest is involved in ongoing innovative reforms and practices in order to meet the demands of its mission statement:

> Quest High School is committed to providing a personalized learning experience in a working partnership with the community to create lifelong learners and successful members of society.

Students are positively affected by the person-centered mission of the school. When asked how attending Quest had influenced their lives, students replied:

Note: References to Carl Rogers' 1962 chapter reflect the page numbers of the chapter as reprinted in this book (pp. 35–51).

Quest has given me the chance to learn a better sense of responsibility and to use it in my everyday life. . . . It's also done something for me no other school would: given me a friend.

—10th grade student

Quest has provided a place for me that is friendly to my idea of what learning should be. It has also given me an environment that is very close to that of a small private school while providing the openness of a public school.

—9th grade student

Quest has helped me to become more responsible, independent, and creative. It has also taught me a lot about what I should expect from others and what others will expect from me in the real world.

—12th grade student

BUILDING TRUST IN SELF AND OTHERS

Quest creates its person-centered environment through three main integrated initiatives, which build trust in self and others. First, the campus is an open school with 180 students that functions around the concept of a community of learners. By open school, I mean that students are free and trusted to work where they need without the restrictions of classrooms. The small-school concept provides the necessary opportunity for personalized learning to occur.

Second, the 180 students belong to "houses," which contain eight families. Each family of 20 students works with a lead facilitator. While at Quest, students remain with the same facilitator and family until they graduate. Each family meets every morning from 7:30–8:00. During this time, students share their goals for the day, work is returned and discussed, school issues are shared, and members of the family voice concerns and talk about issues they feel affect their lives. For example, students decided this year that food services were not adequate at the school. They formed a committee from each family that met with district staff and campus food services. Together, committee members completely transformed menu items and the aesthetics of the dining area. Students also serve on curriculum, discipline, and site-based committees. Family discussions begin with student involvement in the school, and students have strong feelings about these opportunities for dialogue:

> Family discussion is good. Since we choose to go here, we should have some say in what we do. This also makes me feel more important; I feel like I have more power.
>
> —10th grade student

> I really like this school because you can show yourself as an individual instead of just another systematic product of a normal high school.
>
> —10th grade student

Together, staff and students truly accept and trust one another, and this personal relationship leads to significant learning.

For Rogers, trusting of self and others was essential. Being open to experiences was equally important. At Quest, experiencing learning *is* the method of education and the third way that the school creates its person-centered environment. Open, experiential education "has a significant effect on the broad goals of education, including 'cooperation, critical thinking, self-reliance, constructive attitudes, and lifelong learning' [Walberg, 1986] without diminishing the more specific achievement gains of students" (Rogers & Freiberg, 1994, p. 261).

Experiential and inquiry learning at Quest begins with an integrated curriculum and instruction that is thematic and real-world based. Students learn through extended six-week projects called "Exploratories," which are based on the year's "Essential Question," an overarching thematic question that students attempt to answer through exploratory work. Developed by faculty in the past and with future input from students, the Essential Question for 1996–97 was, "What Is Chaos, What Is Order?" For 1997–98 the Essential Question was "How Do We Get from There to Here?" In each Exploratory students engage in activities in both the cognitive and the affective curriculum areas in order to provide an in-depth answer to the Essential Question. During each Exploratory project, students respond to deep and open-ended questions that involve English, social science, science, math, wellness, fine arts, technology, and career education.

DEVELOPING LEARNING COMMUNITIES

The process of becoming a fully functioning person must begin with one's education and experiences in school. This journey can lead to a rich and meaningful life, though Rogers clearly implies that this process of becoming is not an easy task:

> This process of healthy living is not, I am convinced, a life for the fainthearted. It involves the stretching and growing of becoming more and more of one's potentials. It involves the courage to be. It means launching oneself into the stream of life. Yet the deeply exciting thing about human beings is that when the individual is inwardly free, he chooses the process of becoming. (p. 51)

Therefore, it certainly becomes the charge of education to begin this path for each child. Good schools should challenge and stretch each student's mind while providing an environment in which students feel "inwardly free." Education must change its traditional "tourist-like" approach, and begin with the individual child in mind (Freiberg, 1996). "We must trust our feelings and risk the challenges of new experiences. Let's rededicate ourselves to providing learning communities that kids love and that are so rewarding for adults. To accomplish this goal, we must step back and trust our students and ourselves, and give us all the *freedom to learn* (Rogers & Freiberg, 1994, p. 375).

I firmly believe that through person-centered education, Quest students are on the road to becoming the type of fully functioning people whom Rogers strived to develop—an ideal many of us continue to share today.

References

Freiberg, H. J. (1996). From tourists to citizens in the classroom. *Educational Leadership* 54(1), 32–36.

Rogers, C. R., & Freiberg, H. J. (1994). *Freedom to learn.* (3rd ed.). Columbus: Merrill.

Walberg, H. (1986). Synthesis of research on teaching. In M. Wittrock (Ed.), *Handbook of research on teaching* (3rd ed.). New York: Macmillan.

A Response to

"Toward Becoming a Fully Functioning Person"
by Carl R. Rogers

The High School Counselor and the "Fully Functioning Person"

Carolyn A. Jackson • *Scarborough High School, Houston, Texas*

Change is a real phenomenon that most of us brace for, but seldom embrace. As a result we often run from new experiences, or we color them with old perceptions.

Students who have negative experiences in one of the lower grades come to high school expecting to fail. Often by the end of the 9th grade, they have fulfilled this prophecy by failing a grade, becoming pregnant, using drugs, or dropping out. Too often, teachers are part of the prophecy; as a counselor, I see many of these problems every day.

PROVIDING A SAFE HAVEN

I believe that young people's behavioral problems are symptoms of much larger issues. These problems are part of the whole person; therefore, they must emerge and the individual face them before he or she can evolve as a meaningful and productive person. These problems are often defense mechanisms that allow students to cope on a daily basis. As counselors, we must provide a safe haven for our students; as Rogers puts it, the individual needs to realize that he or she is "accepted unconditionally":

> Thus, he becomes acquainted with elements of his experience which have in the past been denied to awareness as too threatening, too

Note: References to Carl Rogers' 1962 chapter reflect the page numbers of the chapter as reprinted in this book (pp. 35–51).

damaging to the structure of the self. He finds himself experiencing these feelings fully, completely, in the relationship, so that for the moment he *is* his fear, or his anger, or his tenderness, or his strength. And as he lives and accepts these widely and varied feelings, in all their degrees of intensity, he discovers that he has experienced *himself*, that he *is* all these feelings. He finds his behavior changing in constructive fashion in accordance with this newly experienced and newly accepted self. He approaches the realization that he no longer needs to fear what experience may hold, but can welcome it freely as a part of his changing and developing self. (p. 38)

Rogers' views on "Toward Becoming a Fully Functioning Person" provide wisdom for constructing meaning in response to the "ills" in education. Before educators can make bold attempts to prepare students for life, we must first work through our *own* baggage. We must query ourselves about our own authenticity and level of functioning. After reflecting on these questions, educators are ready to begin our quest of helping students understand the difficulties that arise in their everyday lives.

TOUCHING CHILDREN'S LIVES

I undertake my expanded relationship with my students with great zeal and enthusiasm. Not only am I a high school counselor, but I am a friend, a mentor, a parent, a teacher. I want to be what is needed at the particular moment. Too often, because of the many demands of the position, counseling can become the shuffling of paper. Counselors must remember that children's lives are embedded in this bureaucracy. We must see each piece of paper as an opportunity for open dialogue.

I eagerly await the arrival of my students for our frequent "morning chats." During our time together, I try to become acquainted with the inner-person by establishing a relaxed environment, one of openness and harmony. In these encounters, I am sometimes fortunate enough to observe students as they find the ability to embrace "change" in themselves and with others.

The acceptance of change allays our fears and concerns about the future. As Rogers writes, "What I will be in the next moment, and what I will do, grow out of the moment, and cannot be predicated in advance either by me or by others."

The two most important services any school can provide for its students is that they feel good about themselves when they enter each morning and when they exit each day. Educators have the potential to provide an environment in which students can embrace the necessary changes in their lives.

Some Basic Propositions of a Growth and Self-Actualization Psychology

A. H. Maslow

This chapter originally appeared in the 1962 ASCD Yearbook, *Perceiving, Behaving, Becoming: A New Focus for Education*.

Some Basic Propositions of a Growth and Self-Actualization Psychology

A. H. Maslow • *Brandeis University*

When the philosophy of man (his nature, his goals, his potentialities, his fulfillment) changes, then everything changes. Not only the philosophy of politics, of economics, of ethics and values, of interpersonal relations and of history itself change, but also the philosophy of education, the theory of how to help men become what they can and deeply need to become.

We are now in the middle of such a change in the conception of man's capacities, potentialities and goals. A new vision is emerging of the possibilities of man and of his destiny, and its implications are many, not only for our conceptions of education, but also for science, politics, literature, economics, religion, and even our conceptions of the nonhuman world.

I think it is finally possible to begin to delineate this view of human nature as a total, single, comprehensive system of psychology even though much of it has arisen as a reaction *against* the limitations (as philosophies of human nature) of the two most comprehensive psychologies now available, behaviorism, or associationism, and classical, Freudian psycho analysis. Finding a single label for it is still a difficult task, perhaps a premature one. I have called it the "holistic-dynamic" psychology to express my conviction about its major roots. Some have called it "organismic," following Goldstein. Sutich and others are calling it the "self-psychology." We shall see. My own guess is that, in a few decades, if it remains suitably eclectic and comprehensive, it will be called simply "psychology."

I think I can be of most service by writing primarily for myself and out of my own work rather than from that of other thinkers, even though I am sure that the areas of agreement among them are very large. A selection of works of this "third force" is listed in the references. Because of space limitation, I will present only some of the major propositions of this point of view, especially those of importance to the educator. In general, I should warn the reader that at many points I am out ahead of the data, sometimes *way* out.

BASIC PROPOSITIONS

1. We have, each one of us, an essential inner nature which is intrinsic, given, "natural," and, usually, very resistant to change.

It makes sense to speak here of the hereditary, constitutional, and very early acquired roots of the *individual* self, even though this biological determination of self is only partial, and far too complex to describe simply. In any case, this is "raw material" rather than finished product, to be reacted to by the person, by his significant others, by his environment, etc.

I include in this essential inner nature instinctoid needs, capacities, talents, anatomical equipment, physiological balances, prenatal and natal injuries, and traumata to the neonatus. Whether defense and coping mechanisms, "style of life," and other characterological traits, all shaped in the first few years of life, should be included, is still a matter for discussion. I would say "yes" and proceed on the assumption that this raw material very quickly starts growing into a self as it meets the world outside and begins to have transactions with it.

2. Each person's inner nature has some characteristics which all other selves have (species-wide) and some which are unique to the person (idiosyncratic). The need for love characterizes every human being that is born (although it can disappear later under certain circumstances). Musical genius, however, is given to very few and these differ markedly from each other in style, e.g., Mozart and Debussy.

3. It is possible to study this inner nature scientifically and objectively (that is, with the right kind of "science") and to discover what it is like (*discover*—not invent or construct). It is also possible to do this subjectively, by inner search and by psychotherapy, and the two enterprises supplement and support each other.

4. Even though weak, this inner nature rarely disappears or dies, in the usual person, in the United States (such disappearance or dying is possible,

however). It persists underground, unconsciously, even though denied and repressed. Like the voice of the intellect, it speaks softly, but it *will* be heard, even if in a distorted form. That is, it has a dynamic force of its own, pressing always for open, uninhibited expression. Effort must be used in its suppression or repression, from which fatigue can result. This force is one main aspect of the "will to health," the urge to grow, the pressure to self-actualization, the quest for one's identity. It is this that makes psychotherapy, education, and self-improvement possible in principle.

5. However, this inner core, or self, grows into adulthood only partly by (objective or subjective) discovery, uncovering and acceptance of what is "there" beforehand. Partly it is also a creation of the person himself. Life is a continual series of choices for the individual in which a main determinant of choice is the person as he already is (including his goals for himself, his courage or fear, his feeling of responsibility, his ego-strength or "will power," etc.). We can no longer think of the person as "fully determined" where this phrase implies "determined only by forces external to the person." The person, insofar as he *is* a real person, is his own main determinant. Every person is, in part, "his own project," and makes himself.

6. No psychological health is possible unless this essential core of the person is fundamentally accepted, loved, and respected by others and by himself (the converse is not necessarily true, i.e., that if the core is respected, etc., then psychological health must result, since other prerequisite conditions must also be satisfied).

The psychological health of the chronologically immature is called healthy growth. The psychological health of the adult is called, variously, self-fulfillment, emotional maturity, individuation, productiveness, self-actualization, etc.

Healthy growth is conceptually subordinate, for it is usually defined now as "growth toward self-actualization," etc. Some psychologists speak simply in terms of one overarching goal or end, or tendency of human development, considering all immature growth phenomena to be only steps along the path to self-actualization (Goldstein, 1939; Rogers & Dymond, 1954).

Self-actualization is defined in various ways, but a solid core of agreement is perceptible. All definitions accept or imply: (a) acceptance and expression of the inner core or self, i.e., actualization of these latent capacities and potentialities, "full functioning," availability of the human and personal essence; and (b) minimal presence of ill health, neurosis, psychosis, of loss or diminution of the basic human and personal capacities.

7. If this essential core (inner nature) of the person is frustrated, denied or suppressed, sickness results, sometimes in obvious forms, sometimes in subtle and devious forms, sometimes immediately, sometimes later. These psychological illnesses include many more than those listed by the American Psychiatric Association. For instance, the character disorders and disturbances are now seen as far more important for the fate of the world than the classical neuroses or even the psychoses. From this new point of view, new kinds of illness are most dangerous, e.g., "the diminished or stunted person," i.e., the loss of any of the defining characteristics of humanness, or personhood, the failure to grow to one's potential; valuelessness (see proposition 19); etc.

That is, general illness of the personality is seen as any falling short of growth, or of self-actualization. And the main source of illness (although not the only one) is seen as frustration of the basic needs, of idiosyncratic potentials, of expression of the self, and of the tendency of the person to grow in his own style, especially in the early years of life.

8. This inner nature, as much as we know of it so far, is definitely not "evil," but is either what we adults in our culture call "good" or else it is neutral. The most accurate way to express this is to say it is "prior to good and evil." There is little question about this if we speak of the inner nature of the infant and child. The statement is much more complex if we speak of the "infant" as he still exists in the adult.

This conclusion is supported by all the truth-revealing and uncovering techniques that have anything to do with human nature: psychotherapy, objective science, subjective science, education, and art. For instance, uncovering therapy lessens hostility, fear, greed, etc., and increases love, courage, creativeness, kindness, altruism, etc., leading us to the conclusion that the latter are "deeper," more natural, and more basic than the former, i.e., that what we call "bad" behavior is lessened or removed by uncovering, while what we call "good" behavior is strengthened and fostered by uncovering.

9. "Evil" behavior has mostly referred to unwarranted hostility, cruelty, destructiveness, "mean" aggressiveness. This we do not know enough about. To the degree that this quality of hostility is instinctoid, mankind has one kind of future. To the degree that it is reactive (a response to bad

treatment), mankind has a very different kind of future. My opinion is that the weight of the evidence so far indicates that *destructive* hostility is reactive, because uncovering therapy reduces it and changes its quality into "healthy" self-affirmation, forcefulness, righteous indignation, etc. In any case, the *ability* to be aggressive and angry is found in all self-actualizing people, who are able to let it flow forth freely when the external situation "calls for" it.

The situation in children is far more complex. At the very least, we know that the healthy child is also able to be justifiably angry, self-protecting, and self-affirming, i.e., reactive aggression. Presumably, then, a child should learn not only how to control his anger, but also how and when to express it.

10. This inner core, even though it is biologically based and instinctoid, is weak rather than strong. It is easily overcome, suppressed, or repressed. It may even be killed off permanently. Humans no longer have instincts in the animal sense—powerful, unmistakable inner voices which tell them unequivocally what to do, when, where, how, and with whom. All that we have left are instinct-remnants. And furthermore, these are weak, subtle, and delicate, very easily drowned out by learning, by cultural expectations, by fear, by disapproval, etc. They are *hard* to know, rather than easy. Authentic selfhood can be defined in part as being able to hear these impulse-voices within oneself, i.e., to know what one really wants or does not want, what one is fit for and what one is *not* fit for, etc.

11. For all these reasons, it is at this time best to bring out and encourage, or, at the very least, to recognize this inner nature, rather than to suppress or repress it. Pure spontaneity consists of free, uninhibited, uncontrolled, trusting, unpremeditated expression of the self, i.e., of the psychic forces, with minimal interference by consciousness. Control, will, caution, self-criticism, measure, deliberateness, are the brakes upon this expression made intrinsically necessary by the laws of the social and natural worlds outside this psychic world, and, secondarily, made necessary by fear of the psyche itself. Speaking in a very broad way, controls upon the psyche, which come from *fear of the psyche*, are largely neurotic or *psychotic*, or not intrinsically or theoretically necessary. (The healthy psyche is not terrible or horrible and therefore does not have to be feared, as it has been for thousands of years. Of course, the *unhealthy* psyche is another story.) This kind of control is usually lessened by psychological health, by

deep psychotherapy, or by any *deeper* self-knowledge and self-acceptance. There are also, however, controls upon the psyche which do not come out of fear, but out of the necessities for keeping it integrated, organized, and unified. And there are also "controls," probably in another sense, which are necessary as capacities are actualized and as higher forms of expression are sought for, e.g., acquisition of skills by the artist, the intellectual, the athlete. But these controls are eventually transcended and become aspects of spontaneity, as they become self.

The balance between spontaneity and control varies, then, as the health of the psyche and the health of the world vary. Pure spontaneity is not long possible because we live in a world which runs by its own nonpsychic laws. It *is* possible in dreams, fantasies, love, imagination, the first stages of creativity, artistic work, intellectual play, free association, etc. Pure control is not permanently possible, for then the psyche dies. Education must be directed then *both* toward cultivation of controls and cultivation of spontaneity and expression. In our culture and at this point in history, it is necessary to redress the balance in favor of spontaneity, the ability to be expressive, passive, unwilled, trusting in processes other than will and control, unpremeditated, creative, etc. But it must be recognized that there have been and will be other cultures and other eras in which the balance was or will be in the other direction.

12. Coordinate with this "acceptance" of the self, of fate, of one's call, is the conclusion that the main path to health and self-fulfillment is via basic need gratification rather than via frustration. This contrasts with the suppressive regime, the mistrust, the control, the policing that is necessarily implied by basic evil in the human depths. Intra-uterine life is completely gratifying and nonfrustrating, and it is now generally accepted that the first year or so of life also had better be primarily gratifying and nonfrustrating. Asceticism, self-denial, deliberate rejection of the demands of the organism, at least in the West, tend to produce a diminished, stunted, or crippled organism, and even in the East, bring self-actualization to very few exceptionally strong individuals.

13. In the normal development of the normal child, it is now known that *most* of the time, if he is given a really free choice, he will choose what is good for his growth. This he does because it tastes good, feels good, gives pleasure or *delight*. This implies that *he* "knows" better than anyone else what is good for him. A permissive regime means not that adults gratify his

needs directly, but make it possible for *him* to gratify his needs and to make his own choices, i.e., let him *be*. It is necessary, in order for children to grow well, that adults have enough trust in them and in the natural processes of growth, i.e., not interfere too much, not *make* them grow, or force them into predetermined designs, but rather *let* them grow and *help* them grow in a Taoistic rather than an authoritarian way.

14. But we know also that the *complete absence* of frustration is dangerous. To be strong, a person must acquire frustration-tolerance, the ability to perceive physical reality as essentially indifferent to human wishes, the ability to love others and to enjoy their need-gratification as well as one's own (not to use other people only as means). The child with a good basis of safety, love, and respect-need-gratification is able to profit from nicely graded frustrations and become stronger thereby. If they are more than he can bear, if they overwhelm him, we call them traumatic, and consider them dangerous rather than profitable.

It is via the frustrating unyieldingness of physical reality and of animals and of other people that we learn about *their* nature, and thereby learn to differentiate wishes from facts (which things wishing makes come true, and which things proceed in complete disregard of our wishes), and are thereby enabled to live in the world and adapt to it as necessary.

We learn also about our own strengths and limits by overcoming difficulties, by straining ourselves to the utmost, by meeting challenge, even by failing. There can be great enjoyment in a great struggle, and this can displace fear.

15. To make growth and self-actualization possible, it is necessary to understand that capacities, organs, and organ systems press to function and express themselves and to be used and exercised, and that such use is satisfying and disuse irritating. The muscular person likes to use his muscles, indeed *has* to use them in order to "feel good" and to achieve the subjective feeling of harmonious, successful, uninhibited functioning (spontaneity) which is so important an aspect of good growth and psychological health. So also for intelligence, for the uterus, the eyes, the capacity to love. Capacities clamor to be used, and cease their clamor only when they *are* well used. That is, capacities are also needs. Not only is it fun to use our capacities, but it is also necessary. The unused capacity or organ can become a disease center or else atrophy, thus diminishing the person.

16. The psychologist proceeds on the assumption that for his purposes

there are two kinds of worlds, two kinds of reality, the natural world and the psychic world, the world of unyielding facts and the world of wishes, hopes, fears, emotions, the world which runs by nonpsychic rules and the world which runs by psychic laws. This differentiation is not very clear except at its extremes, where there is no doubt that delusions, dreams, and free associations are lawful and yet utterly different from the lawfulness of logic and from the lawfulness of the world which would remain if the human species died out. This assumption does not deny that these worlds are related and may even fuse.

I may say that this assumption is acted upon by *many* or *most* psychologists, even though they are perfectly willing to admit that it is an insoluble philosophical problem. Any therapist *must* assume it or give up his functioning. This is typical of the way in which psychologists bypass philosophical difficulties and act "as if" certain assumptions were true even though unprovable, e.g., the universal assumption of "responsibility," "will power," etc.

17. Immaturity can be contrasted with maturity from the motivational point of view, as the process of gratifying the deficiency-needs in their proper order. Maturity, or self-actualization, from this point of view, means to transcend the deficiency-needs. This state can be described then as meta-motivated, or unmotivated (if deficiencies are seen as the only motivations). It can also be described as self-actualizing, Being, expressing, rather than coping. This state of Being, rather than of striving, is suspected to be synonymous with selfhood, with being "authentic," with being a person, with being fully human. The process of growth is the process of *becoming* a person. *Being* a person is different.

18. Immaturity can also be differentiated from maturity in terms of the cognitive capacities (and also in terms of the emotional capacities). Immature and mature cognition have been best described by Werner and Piaget. I wish to add another differentiation, that between D-cognition and B-cognition (D=Deficiency; B=Being.). D-cognition can be defined as the cognitions which are organized from the point of view of basic needs or deficiency-needs and their gratification and frustration. That is, D-cognition could be called selfish cognition, in which the world is organized into gratifiers and frustrators of our own needs, with other characteristics being ignored or slurred. The cognition of the object, in its own right and its own Being, without reference to its need-gratifying or need-frustrating

qualities, that is, without primary reference to its value for the observer or its effects upon him, can be called B-cognition (or self-transcending, or unselfish, or objective cognition). The parallel with maturity is by no means perfect (children can also cognize in a selfless way) but in general, it is mostly true that with increasing selfhood or firmness of personal identity (or acceptance of one's own inner nature) B-cognition becomes easier and more frequent. (This is true even though D-cognition remains for *all* human beings, including the mature ones, the main tool for living-in-the-world.)

To the extent that perception is desire-less and fear-less, to that extent is it more veridical, in the sense of perceiving the true or essential or intrinsic whole nature of the object (without splitting it up by abstraction). Thus the goal of objective and true description of any reality is fostered by psychological health. Neurosis, psychosis, stunting of growth, all are, from this point of view, cognitive diseases as well, contaminating perception, learning, remembering, attending, and thinking.

19. A by-product of this aspect of cognition is a better understanding of the higher and lower levels of love. D-love can be differentiated from B-love on approximately the same basis as D-cognition and B-cognition, or D-motivation and B-motivation. No ideally good relation to another human being, especially a child, is possible without B-love. Especially is it necessary for teaching, along with the Taoistic, trusting attitude that it implies. This is also true for our relations with the natural world, i.e., we can treat it in its own right or we can treat it as if it were there only for our purposes.

20. Though, in principle, growth toward self-actualization is easy, in practice it rarely happens (by my criteria, certainly in less than one percent of the adult population). For this, there are many, many reasons at various levels of discourse, including all the determinants of psychopathology that we now know. We have already mentioned one main cultural reason, i.e., the conviction that man's intrinsic nature is evil or dangerous, and one biological determinant for the difficulty of achieving a mature self, namely that humans no longer have strong instincts.

There is a subtle but extremely important difference between regarding psychopathology as blocking or evasion or fear of growth toward self-actualization and thinking of it in a medical fashion, as akin to invasion from without by tumors, poisons, or bacteria, which have no relationship to the personality being invaded.

21. Growth has not only rewards and pleasures but also many intrinsic pains, and always will have. Each step forward is a step into the unfamiliar and is possibly dangerous. It also means giving up something familiar and good and satisfying. It frequently means a parting and a separation, with consequent nostalgia, loneliness, and mourning. It also often means giving up a simpler and easier and less effortful life, in exchange for a more demanding, more difficult life. Growth forward *is in spite of* these losses and therefore requires courage and strength in the individual, as well as protection, permission, and encouragement from the environment, especially for the child.

22. It is therefore useful to think of growth or lack of it as the resultant of a dialectic between growth-fostering forces and growth-discouraging forces (regression, fear, pains of growth, ignorance, etc.). Growth has both advantages and disadvantages. Non-growing has not only disadvantages but also advantages. The future pulls, but so also does the past. There is not only courage but also fear. The total ideal way of growing healthily is, in principle, to enhance all the advantages of forward growth and all the disadvantages of not-growing, and to diminish all the disadvantages of growth forward and all the advantages of not-growing.

Homeostatic tendencies, "need-reduction" tendencies, and Freudian defense mechanisms are not growth-tendencies, but defensive, pain-reducing postures of the organism. But they are quite necessary and normal (not pathological, necessarily) and are generally prepotent over growth-tendencies.

23. All this implies a naturalistic system of values, a by-product of the empirical description of the deepest tendencies of the human species and of specific individuals (Maslow, 1959). The study of the human being by science or by self-search can discover where he is heading, what his purpose is in life, what is good for him and what is bad for him, what will make him feel virtuous and what will make him feel guilty, why choosing the good is often difficult for him, what the attractions of evil are. (Observe that the word *ought* need not be used. Also such knowledge of man is relative to man only and does not purport to be "absolute.")

24. The state of being without a system of values is psychopathogenic, we are learning. The human being needs a framework of values, a philosophy of life, a religion or religion-surrogate to live by and understand by, in

about the same sense that he needs sunlight, calcium, or love. This I have called the "cognitive need to understand." The value-illnesses which result from valuelessness are called variously anhedonia, anomie, apathy, amorality, hopelessness, cynicism, etc., and can become somatic illness as well. Historically, we are in a value interregnum in which all externally given value systems have proven to be failures (political, economic, religious, etc.), e.g., nothing is worth dying for. What man needs but does not have, he seeks for unceasingly, and he becomes dangerously ready to jump at *any* hope, good or bad. The cure for this disease is obvious. We need a validated, usable system of human values that we can believe in and devote ourselves to (be willing to die for), because they are true rather than because we are exhorted to "believe and have faith." Such an empirically based *Weltanschauung* seems now to be a real possibility, at least in theoretical outline.

Much disturbance in children and adolescents can be understood as a consequence of the uncertainty of adults about their values. As a consequence, many youngsters in the United States live not by adult values, but by adolescent values, which of course are immature, ignorant, and heavily determined by confused adolescent needs. An excellent projection of these adolescent values is the cowboy, or "Western," movie.

25. At the level of self-actualizing, many dichotomies become resolved, opposites are seen to be unities and the whole dichotomous way of thinking is recognized to be immature. For self-actualizing people, there is a strong tendency for selfishness and unselfishness to fuse into a higher, superordinate unity. Work tends to be the same as play; vocation and avocation become the same thing. When duty is pleasant and pleasure is fulfillment of duty, then they lose their separateness and oppositeness. The highest maturity is discovered to include a childlike quality, and we discover healthy children to have some of the qualities of mature self-actualization. The inner-outer split, between self and all else, gets fuzzy and much less sharp, and they are seen to be permeable to each other at the highest levels of personality development.

26. One especially important finding in self-actualizing people is that they tend to integrate the Freudian dichotomies and trichotomies, i.e., the conscious, preconscious, and the unconscious (as well as id, ego, superego). The Freudian "instincts" and the defenses are less sharply set off against each other. The impulses are more expressed and less controlled;

the controls are less rigid, inflexible, anxiety-determined. The superego is less harsh and punishing and less set off against the ego. The primary and secondary cognitive processes are more equally available and more equally valued (instead of the primary processes being stigmatized as pathological). Indeed in the "peak experience" the walls between them tend to fall altogether.

This is in sharp contrast with the classical Freudian position in which these various forces were sharply dichotomized as (a) mutually exclusive, (b) with antagonistic interests, i.e., as antagonistic forces rather than as complementary or collaborating ones.

27. Healthy people are more integrated in another way. In them the conative, the cognitive, the affective, and the motor are less separated from each other, and are more synergic, i.e., working collaboratively without conflict to the same ends. The conclusions of rational, careful thinking are apt to come to the same conclusions as those of the blind appetites. What such a person wants and enjoys is apt to be just what is good for him. His spontaneous reactions are as capable, efficient, and right as if they had been thought out in advance. His sensory and motor reactions are more closely correlated. His sensory modalities are more connected with each other (physiognomical perception). Furthermore, we have learned the difficulties and dangers of those age-old rationalistic systems in which the capacities were thought to be arranged hierarchically, with rationality at the top.

28. This development toward the concept of a healthy unconscious, and of a healthy irrationality, sharpens our awareness of the limitations of purely abstract thinking, of verbal thinking and of analytic thinking. If our hope is to describe the world fully, a place is necessary for pre-verbal, ineffable, metaphorical, primary process, concrete-experience, intuitive and esthetic types of cognition, for there are certain aspects of reality which can be cognized in no other way. Even in science this is true, now that we know (a) that creativity has its roots in the nonrational, (b) that language is and must always be inadequate to describe total reality, (c) that any abstract concept leaves out much of reality, and (d) that what we call "knowledge" (which is usually highly abstract and verbal and sharply defined) often serves to blind us to those portions of reality not covered by the abstraction. That is, it makes us more able to see some things, but *less* able to see other things. Abstract knowledge has its dangers as well as its uses.

Science and education, being too exclusively abstract, verbal, and bookish, do not have enough place for raw, concrete, esthetic experience, especially of the subjective happenings inside oneself. For instance, organismic psychologists would certainly agree on the desirability of more creative education in perceiving and creating art, in dancing, in (Greek style) athletics, and in phenomenological observation.

The ultimate of abstract, analytical thinking is the greatest simplification possible, i.e., the formula, the diagram, the map, the blueprint, certain types of abstract paintings. Our mastery of the world is enhanced thereby, but its richness must be lost as a forfeit, *unless* we learn to value B-cognition, perception-with-love-and-care, free floating attention—all of which enrich the experience instead of impoverishing it.

29. This ability of healthier people to dip into the unconscious and preconscious, to use and value their primary processes instead of fearing them, to accept their impulses instead of always controlling them, to be able to regress voluntarily without fear, turns out to be one of the main conditions of creativity. We can then understand why psychological health is so closely tied up with certain universal forms of creativeness (aside from special talent) as to lead some writers to make them almost synonymous.

This same tie between health and integration of rational and irrational forces (conscious and unconscious, primary and secondary processes) also permits us to understand why psychologically healthy people are more able to enjoy, to love, to laugh, to have fun, to be humorous, to be silly, to be whimsical and fantastic, to be pleasantly "crazy," and in general to permit and value and enjoy emotional experiences in general and peak experiences in particular and to have them more often. And it leads us to the strong suspicion that learning *ad hoc* to be able to do all these things may help the child move toward health.

30. Esthetic perceiving and creating and esthetic peak experiences are seen to be a central aspect of human life and of psychology and education rather than a peripheral one. This is true for several reasons: (a) All the peak experiences are (among other characteristics) integrative of the splits within the person, between persons, within the world, and between the person and the world. Since one aspect of health is integration, the peak experiences are moves toward health and are themselves momentary healths. (b) These experiences are life-validating, i.e., they make life worthwhile. These are certainly an important part of the answer to the

question, "Why don't we all commit suicide?"

31. Self-actualization does not mean a transcendence of all human problems. Conflict, anxiety, frustration, sadness, hurt, and guilt can all be found in healthy human beings. In general, the movement, with increasing maturity, is from neurotic pseudo problems to the real, unavoidable, existential problems inherent in the nature of man (even at his best) living in a particular kind of world. Even though he is not neurotic he may be troubled by real, desirable, and necessary guilt rather than neurotic guilt (which is not desirable or necessary), by an intrinsic conscience (rather than the Freudian superego). Even though he has transcended the problems of Becoming, there remain the problems of Being. To be untroubled when one *should* be troubled can be a sign of sickness. Sometimes, smug people have to be scared "*into* their wits."

32. Self-actualization is not altogether general. It takes place via femaleness or maleness, which are prepotent to general-humanness. That is, one must first be a healthy, femaleness-fulfilled woman before general-human self-actualization becomes possible.

There is also a little evidence that different constitutional types actualize themselves in somewhat different ways (because they have different inner selves to actualize).

33. Another crucial aspect of healthy growth to selfhood is dropping away the techniques used by the child, in his weakness and smallness, for adapting himself to the strong, large, all-powerful, omniscient, godlike adults. He must replace these with the techniques of being strong and independent and of being a parent himself. This involves especially giving up the child's desperate wish for the exclusive, total love of his parents while learning to love others. He must learn to gratify his own needs and wishes, rather than the needs of his parents, and he must learn to gratify them himself, rather than depending upon the parents to do this for him. He must give up being good out of fear and in order to keep their love, and must be good because *he* wishes to be. He must discover his own conscience and give up his internalized parents as a sole ethical guide. All these techniques by which weakness adapts itself to strength are necessary for the child, but immature and stunting in the adult.

34. From this point of view, a society or a culture can be either growth-fostering or growth-inhibiting. The sources of growth and of humanness are essentially within the human person and are not created or invented by

society, which can only help or hinder the development of humanness, just as a gardener can help or hinder the growth of a rosebush, but cannot determine that it shall be an oak tree. This is true even though we know that a culture is a *sine qua non* for the actualization of humanness itself, e.g., language, abstract thought, ability to love; but these exist as potentialities in human germ plasm prior to culture.

This makes theoretically possible a comparative sociology, transcending and including cultural relativity. The "better" culture gratifies all basic human needs and permits self-actualization. The "poorer" cultures do not. The same is true for education. To the extent that it fosters growth toward self-actualization, it is "good" education.

As soon as we speak of "good" or "bad" cultures, and take them as means rather than as ends, the concept of "adjustment" comes into question. We must ask, "What kind of culture or subculture is the 'well adjusted' person well adjusted *to?*" Adjustment is, very definitely, *not* necessarily synonymous with psychological health.

35. The achievement of self-actualization (in the sense of autonomy) paradoxically makes *more* possible the transcendence of self, and of self-consciousness and of selfishness. It makes it *easier* for the person to be homonomous, i.e., to merge himself as a part in a larger whole than himself. The condition of the fullest homonomy is full autonomy, and, to some extent, vice versa—one can attain to autonomy only via successful homonomous experiences (child dependence, B-love, care for others, etc.). It is necessary to speak of levels of homonomy (more and more mature), and to differentiate a "low homonomy" (of fear, weakness, and regression) from a "high homonomy" (of courage and full, self-confident autonomy).

36. An important existential problem is posed by the fact that self-actualized persons (and *all* people in their peak experiences) occasionally live out-of-time and out-of-the-world (atemporal and aspatial), even though mostly they *must* live in the outer world. Living in the inner psychic world (which is ruled by psychic laws and not by the laws of outer-reality), i.e. the world of experience, of emotion, of wishes and fears and hopes, of love, of poetry, art, and fantasy, is different from living in and adapting to the nonpsychic reality which runs by laws the person never made and which are not essential to his nature even though he has to live by them. The person who is not afraid of this inner, psychic world can enjoy it to such an extent that it may be called "heaven" by contrast with the

more effortful, fatiguing, externally responsible world of "reality," of striving and coping, of right and wrong, of truth and falsehood. This is true even though the healthier person can adapt more easily and enjoyably to the "real" world, and has better "reality testing," i.e., does not confuse it with his inner, psychic world.

It seems quite clear now that confusing these inner and outer realities, or having either closed off from experience, is highly pathological. The healthy person is able to integrate them both into his life and therefore has to give up neither, being able to go back and forth voluntarily. The difference is the same as the one between the person who can *visit* the slums and the one who is forced to live there always. (*Either* world is a slum if one cannot leave it.) Then paradoxically that which was sick and pathological and the "lowest" becomes part of the healthiest and "highest" aspect of human nature. Slipping into "craziness" is frightening only for those who are not fully confident of their sanity. Education must help the person to live in both worlds.

37. The foregoing propositions generate a different understanding of the role of action in psychology. Goal-directed, motivated, coping, striving, purposeful action is an aspect or by-product of the necessary transactions between a psyche and a nonpsychic world.

a. The D-need gratifications come from the world outside the person, not from within. Therefore adaptation to this world is made necessary, e.g., reality-testing, knowing the nature of this world, learning to differentiate this world from the inner world, learning the nature of people and of society, learning to delay gratification, learning to conceal what would be dangerous, learning which portions of the world are gratifying and which dangerous or useless for need-gratification, learning the approved and permitted cultural paths to gratification and techniques of gratification.

b. The world is in itself interesting, beautiful, and fascinating. Exploring it, manipulating it, playing with it, contemplating it, enjoying it, are all motivated kinds of action (cognitive, motor, and esthetic needs).

But there is also action which has little or nothing to do with the world, at any rate at first. Sheer expression of the nature or state or powers (*Funktionslust*) of the organism is an expression of Being rather than of striving. And the contemplation and enjoyment of the inner life not only is a kind of "action" in itself but is also antithetical to action in the world, i.e., it produces stillness and cessation of muscular activity. The ability to wait is a special case of being able to suspend action.

38. From Freud we learned that the past exists *now* in the person. Now we must learn, from growth theory and self-actualization theory, that the future also *now* exists in the person in the form of ideals, hopes, goals, unrealized potentials, mission, fate, destiny, etc. One for whom no future exists is reduced to the concrete, to hopelessness, to emptiness. For him, time must be endlessly "filled." Striving, the usual organizer of most activity, when lost, leaves the person unorganized and unintegrated.

Of course, being in a state of Being needs no future, because it is already *there*. Then Becoming ceases for the moment and its promissory notes are cashed in the form of the ultimate rewards, i.e., the peak experiences, in which time disappears.

Selected References

Allport, G. W. (1955). *Becoming: Basic considerations for a psychology of personality.* New Haven, CT: Yale University Press.

Angyal, A. (1941). *Foundations for a science of personality.* New York: Commonwealth Fund.

Fromm, E. (1947). *Man for himself: An inquiry into the psychology of ethics.* New York: Holt, Rinehart, and Winston.

Goldstein, K. (1939). *Organism: A holistic approach to biology derived from pathological data in man.* New York: American Book Co.

Horney, K. (1950). *Neurosis and human growth: The struggle toward self-realization.* New York: W. W. Norton & Co.

Maslow, A. H. (1954). *Motivation and personality.* New York: Harper & Brothers.

Maslow, A. H. (Ed.). (1959). *New knowledge in human values.* New York: Harper & Brothers.

May, R., Angel, E., & Ellenberger, H. F. (Eds.). (1958). *Existence: A new dimension in psychiatry and psychology.* New York: Basic Books.

Moustakas, C. (Ed.). (1956). *The self: Explorations in personal growth.* New York: Harper & Brothers.

Rogers, C. R., & Dymond, R. F. (Eds.). (1954). *Psychotherapy and personality change: Coordinated research studies in the client-centered approach.* Chicago: University of Chicago Press.

Other Publications by the Author

Maslow, A. H. (1954). *Motivation and personality*. New York: Harper & Brothers.

Maslow, A. H. (Ed.). (1959). *New knowledge in human values*. New York: Harper & Brothers.

Maslow, A. H. (1962). *Toward a psychology of being*. Princeton, NJ: D. Van Nostrand.

A Response to

_____

"Some Basic Propositions of a Growth and
Self-Actualization Psychology" by A. H. Maslow

A Look at Maslow's
"Basic Propositions"

Alfie Kohn • _Belmont, Massachusetts_

Abraham Maslow was a bundle of paradoxes. After writing a popular text on abnormal psychology, he turned to—and virtually initiated—the serious study of healthy people. He apprenticed under some of the leading behaviorists, he was psychoanalyzed for years, yet he shaped a Third Force in psychology that explicitly repudiated behaviorism and psychoanalysis. The anecdotes compiled by his biographer (Hoffman, 1988) suggest a man both gentle and intolerant, timid and arrogant. He dreamt of a new society but recoiled from political activism; he was an atheist enthralled by the possibility of transcendent experiences.

Paradox was a hallmark of his theories as well as his life. Self-actualized people, Maslow told us, transcend dichotomies and resolve oppositions (proposition 25, p. 83). They are not entirely this nor that, and they realize the world isn't either. Thus, it seemed appropriate when, in college, I first drank in Maslow's books, to find myself decidedly ambivalent about what he had to say. I wrote papers taking him to task for certain ideas, yet his broader vision for psychology enthralled me and became part of me. With the affective charge having abated somewhat, with a quieter affirmation here and a more muted objection there, I feel much the same way a couple of decades later.

_____

Note: References to Abraham Maslow's 1962 chapter reflect the page numbers of the chapter as reprinted in this book (pp. 71–90).

A CLOSER LOOK AT "SELF-ACTUALIZATION"

The specific characteristics that Maslow attributed to the self-actualized individual seem less important to me than the fact that he paid attention to growing, mature, fully functioning people in the first place. Psychology had hitherto been much more interested in pathology, and when mental health was discussed at all, it was implicitly understood in terms of adaptation to social norms, such that "healthy" and "normal" were regarded as interchangeable. Maslow argued that "adjustment is, very definitely, *not* necessarily synonymous with psychological health" (proposition 34, pp. 86–87). (Thus, confronted with "proof" that an instructional technique, or discipline system, in the classroom is effective, we might well ask, "Effective at what?"—knowing that the answer may have more to do with adaptation and adjustment, with the perpetuation of the status quo, than with genuine health.) In addition to challenging the view of health as adaptation, Maslow (along with Marie Jahoda, Erich Fromm, and other humanists) also took issue with the medical model's view of health as tantamount to the absence of illness, insisting instead on a *positive* definition of health—one that specified what human beings are like at their best.

The call for psychologists to investigate health was not a dispassionate recommendation for Maslow, analogous to asking that more attention be paid to this or that developmental stage. Rather, it reflected a belief that there *was* much about us humans that was healthy, admirable, worth celebrating. This conviction, shared by Carl Rogers and others, has provided a contemporary counterpoint to the bleak view of our species offered by Freud, Hobbes, and the doctrine of Original Sin. I found the humanists' benign perspective refreshing when I first encountered it, and I subsequently discovered a cache of empirical evidence that, to some extent at least, corroborated what Maslow and others had been saying (Kohn, 1990). More recently, I have become interested in exposing and criticizing the cynical assumptions about children that underlie mainstream arguments for classroom management (Kohn, 1996, chap. 1) and character education (Kohn, 1997).

Still, I have my reservations. In good Maslovian form, I wonder whether Humans as Good is just the mirror image of Humans as Bad, equally reductive and ultimately as unconvincing. But what is the alternative position? That we are somewhere in between? Maybe. That we are both good and evil? If this is closer to the truth, it suggests that we must come to terms with a full range of human impulses and capacities, as has been argued by Rollo May (1982), perhaps the most incisive and complicated thinker associated with humanistic psychology. Ultimately, though, the alternative to Good vs. Evil may be not that we are both, but that we are neither—at least if good and evil are construed as givens.

The existentialist tradition, which May (1958) single-handedly introduced to American psychology, calls into question the idea of a fixed human nature, emphasizing instead how much we determine our own nature and, more to the point, how we decide not just *whether* to be good but what it *means* to call something "good" in the first place. Both who we are and how we should act are more within the realm of human choice than we sometimes care to acknowledge. Biological determinism is therefore no less problematic just because we attribute agreeable qualities (e.g., altruism, the capacity to be self-actualizing) rather than disagreeable qualities (e.g., aggression, selfishness) to our essential make-up. The former characteristics may be nice, but that does not make it any less problematic to think of them as "natural" if, in fact, we are creators as much as discoverers, composers as much as archaeologists.

Maslow gave some credence to this idea (proposition 5, p. 75), but the bulk of his life's work was informed by precisely the opposite conviction. Healthy people, he believed, are those who actualize—that is, make real—what they already are. He spoke frequently of an "inner nature," and saw psychotherapy as an attempt to help "the person to *discover* his Identity, his Real Self, in a word, his own subjective biology, which he can *then* proceed to actualize, to 'make himself,' to 'choose' " (Maslow, 1976, p. 179).

Among the problems with this position is that it commits what philosophers since Hume have identified as the "naturalistic fallacy," which refers to the attempt to derive a value from a fact. Just agreeing that something is part of human nature—or, for that matter, that it is true to *my* nature—does not in and of itself permit us to say that this thing is desirable, good, or healthy. Thus, Maslow made a very basic conceptual error when he declared that "the word *ought* need not be used" and we can rely on "a naturalistic system of values, a by-product of the empirical description of the deepest tendencies of the human species and of specific individuals" (proposition 23, p. 82). In another essay, he stated that

the best way for a person to discover what he ought to do is to find out
who and what he is, because the path to ethical and value decisions,
to wiser choices, to oughtness, is via "isness". . . . Many problems simply disappear; many others are easily solved by knowing what is in
conformity with one's nature, what is suitable and right (1976,
pp. 106–107).

In fact, the problems—and the necessity of demonstrating why something
is good or ought to be done—do not disappear at all. They are just conven-
iently avoided when we blithely invite people to "find their inner selves."

Look it at it this way: If Maslow says it is good to be who we really are,
that statement is offered either as an analytic truth or an empirical truth. If
it's analytical, he is basically saying it is true by definition, that "in conformity with one's nature" is part of the *meaning* of words like "right" or
"healthy." This requires some justification; one can't, after all, prove a contention just by defining it to be true. If his claim is empirical, though, then
he is suggesting that science can show that people do in fact move toward
health or goodness (given certain facilitating environmental conditions),
or that what is in conformity with one's nature does in fact turn out to be
healthy. In this case, Maslow obviously has some independent standard of
what constitutes health or goodness, some value by which our actions can
be judged. M. Brewster Smith, a critic from within humanistic psychology,
saw the latter as the only way to read Maslow:

> His empirical definition of psychological health or self-actualization
> thus rests, at root, on his own implicit values that underlie this global
> judgment. The array of characteristics that he reports must then be re-
> garded not as an empirical description of the fully human . . . but
> rather as an explication of his implicit conception of the fully human,
> of his orienting frame of human values. . . . I like them, but that is be-
> side the point (Smith, 1973, p. 24).

Of course, there is nothing wrong with making value judgments about
what humans ought to be like—only with declaring after the fact that they
are not really value judgments at all but are contained within factual statements about what we *are* like.

Then there is the painfully obvious question: How can we defend the "natural" tendencies of a species that commits unspeakable atrocities with some regularity? The humanists' only move here is to discount the bad stuff as not reflective of our deepest tendencies, as not being in tune with our *real* nature. But how do we know what is deepest or most real? Have we, once again, simply defined anything evil as less deep or true than the good? How can such a decision be defended? The humanists offer a key caveat, of course, which is that health consists of what people freely choose "under certain conditions that we have learned to call good"; the choices that reveal our nature are those made by "sound adults or children who are not yet twisted and distorted" (Maslow, 1970, pp. 272, 278). But these value-laden qualifiers undermine any claim that we can skip the oughts and proceed directly from facts to values[1]; they essentially prove Smith (1973, p. 25) correct when he concludes that "our biology cannot be made to carry our ethics as Maslow would have it."

NEEDS

If the specifics of Maslow's definition of health become more problematic upon closer inspection, his willingness to devote serious attention to the subject may be his more admirable, and lasting, legacy. Exactly the same is true of his contribution to the study of what people need. Maslow proposed that the extent to which our needs are met can predict how well we function, and this insight helps us understand what happens in families, classrooms, workplaces, and society more generally. Particularly with respect to children, we can predict that more developmentally appropriate and constructive practices will follow when our first question is "What do kids need, and how can we meet those needs?" as opposed to "How can we get kids to do what we tell them?" Any number of thinkers have made a similar point—one thinks of the motivational psychologists Edward Deci and Richard Ryan or the psychiatrist William Glasser, for example—but back in the 1940s Maslow helped all of us to grasp the importance of ensuring, as he later put it, "that the child's basic psychological needs are satisfied" (1976, p. 183).

---

[1] I believe these objections also apply to Lawrence Kohlberg's (1971) cleverer and more self-conscious attempt to do essentially the same thing with his stage theory of moral development.

Maslow explicitly repudiated the homeostatic (or tension-reduction) view that says we, like all organisms, are motivated chiefly to satisfy our inborn needs in an effort to return to a condition of rest or stasis. Maslow believed that "gratification of one need and its consequent removal from the center of the stage brings about not a state of rest . . . but rather the emergence into consciousness of another 'higher' need" (Maslow, 1968, p. 30). The higher needs are distinguished, among other things, by seeming more like desires than compulsions.

This proposition simultaneously challenges the Freudian model, which is essentially homeostatic, and the behaviorist model, which sees us as no more than "repertoires of behaviors" that are, in turn, fully determined by "environmental contingencies." The humanistic view holds that we are not at the mercy of outside forces; our motivations often come from within and, moreover, have a freely chosen component to them. ("The self-actualizer's wishes and plans are the primary determiners, rather than stresses from the environment" [1968, p. 35].) The goal is not stasis but continual growth, not a respite from needs but a shift to different kinds of needs and more joy in satisfying them.

Maslow distinguished between deficiency and growth motivation, between need-interested and need-disinterested perception, and between D (for Deficiency) love and B (for Being) love (propositions 18 and 19, pp. 80–81). I have found this set of distinctions both provocative and useful in thinking about a range of issues, notwithstanding the inherent limitations of dualities. Truly, some people see what they need to see, while others are more successful at encountering a new idea or situation without construing it as a means to their own ends, without filtering it through their own emotional hurts and histories. Some people attach themselves to others with a desperation suggesting D-love, much as a starving person would approach a plate of food, while others have the emotional freedom to appreciate others for who they are, feeling more flexible and autonomous, less driven and less likely to turn others into something they aren't. The same basic distinction can be applied to how one approaches ideas—a purer B-cognition presumably being one goal of education—or even to one's sense of humor. Consistent with the B vs. D formulation, for example, one might argue that competitiveness is properly understood as a deficiency-motivated trait: being good at an activity may be something we choose to do, but winning is experienced as something we *have* to do, psychologically speaking (Kohn, 1986, p. 101). Tragically, competition exacerbates rather than satisfies that lower-level need.

Again, though, the ambivalence: while making use of Maslow's framework, I have found myself wincing at its epistemological implications. The very idea of "need-free perception," suggesting that healthy individuals can see things (and people) as they really are, derives from Maslow's straight-faced talk about "the world of unyielding facts" (proposition 16, pp. 79–80). It is also a correlative of his assertion that it is possible for psychologists to study our "inner nature scientifically and objectively (that is, with the right kind of 'science') and to discover what it is like (*discover*—not invent or construct)" (proposition 3, p. 74). This brand of naive empiricism has been rudely displaced by 20th century physics, to say nothing of modern constructivism. No matter how healthy we may be, "knowledge does not reflect an 'objective' ontological reality, but exclusively an ordering and organization of a world constituted by our experience" (von Glaserfeld, 1984, p. 24). Progressive educators may be attracted both to Maslow's humanism and to a constructivist understanding of learning, but it is important to acknowledge that the two cannot be entirely reconciled.

Where Maslow gets into more trouble is where his theory gets more specific (and more famous): the well-known triangle on which needs are arrayed. Here the two-stage hierarchy of needs—deficiency and growth—is supplanted by a five-stage hierarchy as follows: At the bottom are physiological needs, which are "prepotent," meaning that they must be satisfied first. When people get food and other bodily necessities, they are then concerned about safety. After safety comes the need for belongingness or love, then esteem or achievement, and finally, at the top of the triangle, comes the need for self-actualization, which he defined as "the desire to become more and more what one idiosyncratically is, to become everything that one is capable of becoming" (Maslow, 1970, p. 46). (Incidentally, in the revised edition to his basic text on motivation, published the year he died, Maslow made it clear that he believed "self-actualization does not occur in young people" [p. xx].)

Before mentioning some problems with the hierarchy of needs, we should take a moment to clear up a confusion that is not Maslow's fault. Some people, casually invoking his theory, declare that it is appropriate and even necessary to provide extrinsic inducements (notably, rewards) to an individual, because only later will he or she be ready to "move up" to the level of intrinsic motivation. This formulation is based on several errors. First, it assumes that because intrinsic motivation is desirable, it must be a higher need in the sense that it appears at a later stage of development. In fact, however, Maslow's entire theory of motivation and the whole range of needs it embraces (including the need for self-actualization) could be said to be intrinsic, or part of who we are. We do not always find ourselves in environments that meet these needs and fulfill our potential, but intrinsic motivation, seen as a function of these needs, is present from the start.

What is not there from the start, however, is an extrinsic orientation. There is a profound difference between the things we need (e.g., food, money, approval) and the deliberate use of these things *as rewards* to induce people to behave in a certain way. Those who are controlled with rewards may well come to lose interest in what they have been rewarded for doing (Kohn, 1993) and thereafter may seem extrinsically oriented. But this does not mean that a dependence on (or an expectation of) extrinsic rewards is prepotent over intrinsic, in Maslow's language. In fact, one study of nearly 800 employed adults found "no evidence that workers must learn to appreciate or need intrinsic satisfaction. . . . Extrinsic rewards become an important determinant of overall job satisfaction only among workers for whom intrinsic rewards are relatively unavailable" (Gruenberg, 1980, p. 268). The same may be said of students who appear to be dependent on extrinsic rewards such as grades, stickers, pizza, and praise: what they really needed from the beginning simply wasn't available.

The concept of intrinsic motivation is generally traced back to the work of Robert White (on competence), Richard deCharms (on self-determination), and finally to Harry Harlow, who was apparently the first to use the term in 1950. Maslow, interestingly, was Harlow's first doctoral student some two decades before Harlow and his colleagues discovered that rhesus monkeys not only learned how to operate a mechanical puzzle in the absence of food rewards, but that the introduction of rewards "seriously disrupted the efficient puzzle solution which they had repeatedly demonstrated previously" (Harlow et al., 1950, p. 231). Maslow's name does not appear prominently in most accounts of intrinsic motivation, but there is no doubt that his personality theory helped set the stage for an understanding of the concept. For what it's worth, I'm certain that my own interest in the topic was indirectly an outgrowth of my immersion in Maslow's work sometime earlier.

Let us stipulate, then, that intrinsic motivation is part of Maslow's legacy and that misunderstandings of the "need" for extrinsic motivators are not his fault. Nevertheless, there are real problems with his hierarchy of needs, beginning with the slipperiness of his terms and the difficulty of demonstrating empirically whether or not he was right. It is not just that Maslow was "out ahead of the data," as he himself put it, but that it is virtually impossible to test his theory:

> For example, what behavior should or should not be included in each need category? How can a need be gratified out of existence? What does dominance of a given need mean? What are the conditions under which the theory is operative? How does the shift from one need to another take place? Do people also go down the hierarchy as they go up in it? Is there an independent hierarchy for each situation, or do people develop a general hierarchy for all situations? What is the time span for the unfolding of the hierarchy? These and similar questions are not answered by Maslow and are open for many interpretations. The most problematic aspect of Maslow's theory, however, is that . . . it is not clear what is meant by the concept of need. (Wahba and Bridwell, 1976, p. 234)

To the extent one *can* meaningfully derive testable hypotheses from Maslow's theory, moreover, there is serious reason to think it was wrong. First, the underlying assumption is remarkably deterministic, and one could argue that "what we choose to do depends more on our ethics than on satisfying needs" (Maccoby, 1988, p. 32). If our actions are not in fact driven by a progressive unfolding of inborn needs, then the accuracy—or at least the functional relevance—of the theory is called into question. Second, while it may be intuitively plausible to talk about safety needs, belongingness needs, and so on, "there is no clear evidence that human needs are classified in five distinct categories, or that these categories are structured in a special hierarchy" (Wahba and Bridwell, 1976, p. 224). In fact, there is some evidence to the contrary. Finally, it has never been shown that one need triggers the next in the way Maslow described. If he was right, the satisfaction of a given need—accepting for the sake of the argument that a need can ever really be "satisfied"—should cause that need to subside and also cause the next need in the hierarchy to become more salient. Attempts to demonstrate this, however, have generally failed (e.g., Hall & Nougaim, 1968; Lawler & Suttle, 1972).

The subjects in much of the research on this topic have been corporate managers, possibly limiting the generalizability of the negative findings; what's more, the studies have been plagued by a number of methodological limitations (see Wicker et al., 1993). But even the data that do appear to be supportive may not rescue the theory as a whole. It can be shown that people think less about food once they are fed, but that doesn't demonstrate that the same principle operates with higher needs. It can be shown that corporate employees start out being preoccupied with safety needs and later become more concerned about achievement, but this may be a function of changing social roles or situations rather than proof of some inherent relationship among innate needs that plays out automatically.

Once the empirical basis for Maslow's hierarchy has been challenged, one is free to identify and question the values that led him to arrange these needs in the order he did. That Maslow seems to regard the need for love or affiliation as "lower" than the need for self-actualization or even achievement seems to suggest that the desire to connect with others is "some sort of irritant that needs fixing so that people will be free to focus on more important things such as achievement and success" (Sergiovanni, 1994, pp. 65–66). One has difficulty imagining this particular hierarchy being proposed by a female or Asian psychologist, for example.

Maslow has been faulted for "an atomistic view of the self" (Geller, 1982, p. 69), for his premise that we "achieve full humanness through an intense affair with the self" (Aron, 1977/1986, p. 99).[2] But even those who are sympathetic to the individualism that undergirds his writings, including his equation of health with *self*-actualization, ought to keep in mind that this is the worldview of a particular historical period and a particular

---

[2]Aron's essay is reprinted in *Politics and Innocence*, a fascinating collection devoted to the social and political implications of humanistic psychology. Contributions by Walter Nord and Allan R. Buss, in particular, explore the conservative and individualistic implications of humanistic psychology and especially of Maslow's work. As Buss (1979/1986, p. 140) puts it, "A theory that disposes one to focus more upon individual freedom and development rather than the larger social reality, works in favor of maintaining that social reality."

set of cultural assumptions. Maslow was sufficiently schooled in anthropology (and sufficiently influenced by Ruth Benedict) to be cautious about explicitly claiming his observations were universal truths (e.g., see Maslow, 1970, pp. 54–55), yet much of his work is presented as being a description of human nature. Anyone enamored of self-actualization theory would do well to remember what Clifford Geertz observed:

> The Western conception of the person as a bounded, unique, more or less integrated motivational and cognitive universe, a dynamic center of awareness, emotion, judgment, and action organized into a distinctive whole and set contrastively against both other such wholes and against its social and natural background, is, however incorrigible it may seem to us, a rather peculiar idea within the context of the world's cultures. (Geertz, 1983, p. 59)

MASLOW ON EDUCATION

Maslow had remarkably little to say on the subject of education. His essay in *Perceiving, Behaving, Becoming* did not pay much attention to what happens in schools despite the fact that he was writing it for ASCD, and there is little evidence of systematic thought about pedagogical matters in an article he wrote six years later for the *Harvard Educational Review* (reprinted in Maslow 1976, chap. 13). His few paragraphs on the subject consisted of a call for education to foster "growth toward self-actualization" (proposition 34, pp. 86–87), "learning of the heart" (Maslow 1970, p. 282), "learning who you are," "being able to hear your inner voices" (Maslow, 1976, p. 177), and for education to "refreshen consciousness so that we are continually aware of the beauty and wonder of life" (p. 183). He thought there should be more emphasis on creativity and developing a "healthy unconscious" (proposition 28, pp. 84–85), and more concern, at least in our culture, with "spontaneity, the ability to be expressive, passive, unwilled . . ." (proposition 11, pp. 77–78). By contrast, schools were said to place too much emphasis on "purely abstract thinking" (proposition 28) and "implanting the greatest number of facts into the greatest possible number of children" (Maslow, 1976, p. 173).

When asked about education, Maslow tended to think primarily about the college years—understandably, because he spent most of his life in universities. He was dismayed at the prevailing preoccupation with "means, i.e., grades, degrees, credits, diplomas, rather than with ends, i.e., wisdom, understanding, good judgment, good taste" (Maslow, 1970, p. 282). He wrote about students so driven by "extrinsic rewards" that they could not fathom why anyone would read a book that wasn't required for a course, and he remarked that learning itself was so little valued that "leaving college before the completion of one's senior year is considered to be a waste of time by the society and a minor tragedy by parents" (Maslow, 1976, pp. 174–175). By way of contrast, he told a story about Upton Sinclair:

> When Sinclair was a young man, he found that he was unable to raise the tuition money needed to attend college. Upon careful reading of the college catalogue, however, he found that if a student failed a course, he received no credit for the course, but was obliged to take another course in its place. The college did not charge the student for the second course, reasoning that he had already paid once for his credit. Sinclair took advantage of this policy and got a free education by deliberately failing all his courses. (pp. 174–175)

The little that Maslow did write on education will likely continue to elicit enthusiasm among progressives and derision among traditionalists. To be sure, Maslow's message is not well suited to an era that seems ever more determined to judge schools on the basis of standardized test scores and that ratchets up standards to make students more "competitive." But even those of us who nod at Maslow's remarks about extrinsic rewards (and smile at the Sinclair anecdote) may be forgiven for finding all the earnest talk about spontaneity and inner voices to be rather less than helpful. Authenticity never goes out of date, but Maslow's declarations are sometimes so sweeping and simplistic as to provoke a twinge of embarrassment, as, for example, when he informs educators that addicts "will give up drugs easily if you offer them instead some meaning to their lives" (Maslow, 1976, p. 180) or that even when "parents convey their own distorted patterns of behavior to the child . . . if the teacher's are healthier and stronger, the children will imitate these instead" (p. 181).

There is very little of substance or specificity in Maslow's writings to guide teachers through the exigencies of life in real classrooms. Only once that I am aware of did he even acknowledge the structural barriers that might constrain teachers from encouraging peak experiences in their students.[3] In general, while Maslow's thoughts about psychology may be indirectly relevant to education, just as they may be indirectly relevant to architecture or any other field, he was clearly not steeped in the particulars of life at school or how children learn.

On the other hand, educators absorb and reflect a set of assumptions about who we are as human beings and what we can (and ought to) become. Maslow's optimism, his tireless attention to growth and health, and his analysis of motivation and needs collectively define a psychological perspective that is richer, deeper, and more heuristic than the behaviorism that captivated Maslow himself at age 20 but which he later transcended. We might take issue with any number of his ideas while still finding his conception of human potential a basis for lively discussion and a source of energy and inspiration.

References

Aron, A. (1977/1986). Maslow's other child. Reprinted in *Politics and innocence: A humanistic debate* (pp. 98–111). Dallas: Saybrook. (Originally published 1977)

Buss, A. (1979/1986). Humanistic psychology as liberal ideology: The socio-historical roots of Maslow's theory of self-actualization. Reprinted in *Politics and innocence: A humanistic debate* (pp. 136–148). Dallas: Saybrook. (Originally published 1979)

Geertz, C. (1983). From the native's point of view. In *Local knowledge*. New York: Basic Books.

Geller, L. (1982). The failure of self-actualization theory: A critique of Carl Rogers and Abraham Maslow. *Journal of Humanistic Psychology, 22*(2), 56–73.

Gruenberg, B. (1980). The happy worker: An analysis of educational and occupational differences in determinants of job satisfaction. *American Journal of Sociology, 86,* 247–271.

Hall, D. T., & Nougaim, K. E. (1968). An examination of Maslow's need hierarchy in an organizational setting. *Organizational Behavior and Human Performance, 3,* 12–35.

Harlow, H. F., Harlow, M. K., & Meyer, D. R. (1950). Learning motivated by a manipulation drive. *Journal of Experimental Psychology, 40,* 228–234.

---

[3]"Of course, with the traditional model of 35 children in one classroom and a curriculum of subject matter to be gotten through in a given period of time, the teacher is forced to pay more attention to orderliness and lack of noise than [to] making learning a joyful experience" (Maslow, 1976, p. 181).

Hoffman, E. (1988). *The right to be human: A biography of Abraham Maslow*. Los Angeles: Jeremy P. Tarcher.

Kohlberg, L. (1971). From *is* to *ought*: How to commit the naturalistic fallacy and get away with it in the study of moral development. In T. Mischel, (Ed.), *Cognitive development and epistemology*. New York: Academic Press.

Kohn, A. (1986). *No contest: The case against competition*. Boston: Houghton Mifflin.

Kohn, A. (1990). *The brighter side of human nature: Altruism and empathy in everyday life*. New York: Basic Books.

Kohn, A. (1993). *Punished by rewards: The trouble with gold stars, incentive plans, A's, praise, and other bribes*. Boston: Houghton Mifflin.

Kohn, A. (1996). *Beyond discipline: From compliance to community*. Alexandria, VA: ASCD.

Kohn, A. (1997, February). How not to teach values: A critical look at character education. *Phi Delta Kappan*, 429–439.

Lawler, E. E., III, & Suttle, J. L. (1972). A causal correlational test of the need hierarchy concept. *Organizational Behavior and Human Performance, 7*, 265–287.

Maccoby, M. (1988). *Why work: leading the new generation*. New York: Simon and Schuster.

Maslow, A. H. (1962). "Some basic propositions of a growth and self-actualization psychology." In A. W. Combs (Ed.), 1962 ASCD yearbook, *Perceiving, behaving, becoming: A new focus for education* (pp. 34–49). Alexandria, VA: ASCD.

Maslow, A. H. (1968). *Toward a psychology of being*. (2nd ed.). New York: D. Van Nostrand.

Maslow, A. H. (1970). *Motivation and personality*. (2nd ed.). New York: Harper & Row.

Maslow, A. H. (1976). *The farther reaches of human nature*. New York: Penguin.

May, R. (1958). The origins and significance of the existential movement in psychology and contributions of existential psychotherapy. In R. May, E. Angel, & H. F. Ellenberger, (Eds.), *Existence: A new dimension in psychiatry and psychology*. New York: Touchstone.

May, R. (1982, Summer). The problem of evil: An open letter to Carl Rogers. *Journal of Humanistic Psychology, 22*, 10–21.

Sergiovanni, T. (1994). *Building community in schools*. San Francisco: Jossey-Bass.

Smith, M. B. (1973). On self-actualization. *Journal of Humanistic Psychology, 13*(2), 17–33.

von Glaserfeld, E. (1984). An introduction to radical constructivism. In P. Watzlawick, (Ed.), *The invented reality*. New York: Norton.

Wahba, M. A., & Bridwell, L. G. (1976). Maslow reconsidered: A review of research on the need hierarchy theory. *Organizational behavior and human performance, 15*, 212–240.

Wicker, F. W., Brown, G., Wiehe, J. A., Hagen, A. S., & Reed, J. L. (1993). On reconsidering Maslow: An examination of the deprivation/domination proposition. *Journal of Research in Personality, 27*, 118–133.

A Response to
_____

"*Some Basic Propositions of a Growth and
Self-Actualization Psychology*" *by A. H. Maslow*

Maslow and a Place Called School

Christopher Day • *University of Nottingham, England*
Dolf van Veen • *Hogeschool van Amsterdam, The Netherlands*

S elf-actualization in education today has become increasingly problematic for teachers, teacher educators, and learners alike. The iron
fist of accountability, competencies, quality control, and performance indicators has closed over the kinds of creativity that personal and
professional autonomy permit. Abraham Maslow's visions have become,
for many, lost in the "busyness" of survival. New technologies, fragmenta-
tion of values, disillusionment with political process, and intensification
of teacher work standards have added to the constraints of ever crowding
classrooms and deprofessionalization identified more than 35 years ago
(Jackson, 1968).

The world of today is different if not in substance then certainly in pace
and direction to that experienced by Maslow when he wrote "Some Basic
Propositions of a Growth and Self-Actualization Psychology." So, are his
proposals still relevant? It is not our purpose to analyze all 38 of his propositions here. Rather, we will focus on how they interact with issues of teaching and learning within contexts that show few signs of promising success
for all—whether that success is measured by academic achievements or
dispositions to lifelong learning, which many believe are key to productive
employment, economic success, and personal fulfillment.

_____

Note: References to Abraham Maslow's 1962 chapter reflect the page numbers of the chapter as
reprinted in this book (pp. 71–90).

TOWARD SELF-ACTUALIZATION AND GROWTH

We turn to Maslow's view of our inner nature—shaped in part by personal history, in part by interaction with our various physical, emotional, intellectual, and spiritual environments. The key to successful management of learning and growth must lie not only in good teaching, but in teaching that is clear in its moral purposes. That is, these purposes must be for the betterment of students rather than, for example, the "dumbing down" of content as a means of containment. Good teaching is underpinned not only by caring, skilled application of technique, possession, and communication of appropriate knowledge, but also by interventions that are based upon a keen awareness of change. Yet in this area, Maslow has little to offer. Indeed, as Alfie Kohn writes in this volume, there is "very little of substance or specificity . . . to guide teachers through the exigencies of life in real classrooms" (p. 102).

School systems around the world today are the subject of unprecedented surveillance by governments, media, and the public. These groups are anxious to raise student achievement in the mistaken belief that high test results in a relatively narrow range of subjects directly affect the health of the economy. Teachers are at the sharp end of such surveillance, and evidence increasingly indicates that more teachers work longer hours, suffer from stress, and experience disenchantment than at any point previously. With self-esteem and self-confidence at a low ebb, survival is a primary concern.

Some might argue that Maslow's purpose was not to offer teachers this type of direction. The fact that so many elementary school teachers in particular espouse his pyramid model of psychological growth is testimony enough to the value of his contributions to teaching and learning. It could be argued with force that Maslow's notion of education as being directed toward "cultivation of controls, cultivation of spontaneity, and expression," (p. 78) and of the balance needing to be redressed in favor of spontaneity is as true today as it was then. Alongside this notion, the main path to health and self-fulfillment is via needs gratification, rather than frustration experienced through "mistrust . . . control . . . policing" (p. 78).

Maslow's assertion that "much disturbance in children and adolescents can be understood as a consequence of the uncertainty of adults about their values" (p. 83) is of vital importance in a future fraught with uncertainties of all kinds. Of all adults, teachers are the only group charged with the education of students' values, whether directly by their teaching or indirectly in classroom relationships through which values are transmitted and negotiated. Because both being and becoming a person are central to continuing learning for students and their teachers, both are involved in change. And, as Maslow asserts, growth not only has rewards and pleasures but also many intrinsic pains. It "often means giving up a simpler and easier . . . life, in exchange for a more demanding, more difficult life" (p. 82). Growth, therefore, requires "courage and strength in the individual as well as protection, permission, and encouragement from the environment, especially for the child" (p. 82).

Yet, Maslow's argument that life is "a continual series of choices for the individual in which a main determinant of choice is the person as he already is" (p. 75) might today seem somewhat naive rather than visionary. In our experience, self-actualization that implies "acceptance and expression of the inner core or self," and a "minimal presence of ill-health, neurosis, psychosis, or loss of diminution of the basic human and personal capacities" (pp. 75–76) is only possible, in our experience, temporarily for a few rather than permanently for many. Moreover, "survival," like self-actualization, is a relative term that will have cultural-specific connotations.

Children and adults in socially and economically deprived environments characterized by conflict, poverty, injustice, and unemployment might justifiably not be expected to become self-actualized. Indeed, self-actualization itself might be seen as a positively undesirable goal in these circumstances. Health too is a relative concept, culture- and even individual-specific. While Maslow implies an understanding of this in his 31st proposition—that conflict, anxiety, frustration, sadness, hurt, and guilt can all be found in healthy human beings (p. 86)—his is a selective vision of self-actualization.

CHANGE REALITY OR CHANGE MYTHOLOGY?

Maslow's distinction between being a person (synonymous with selfhood, being authentic) and becoming a person (the process of growth) returns us to the theme of change, which is at the heart of educational purposes. Two of his points are highly relevant to current policy and practice contexts of schools: (1) his plea for integration between rational and non-rational forces, and (2) his argument that autonomy is closely related to the achievement of self-actualization, while needing to be applied in particular contexts. Should preservice teacher education, for example, be controlled through a national curriculum (as in England), in which technical craft cultures, content knowledge, and classroom competencies dominate? Should continuing professional development opportunities for teachers continue to consist mainly of short-burst skills training related to immediate demands of the teacher's school role or classroom pedagogy needs as defined by policymakers and administrators? Are the sole needs of teachers technical competence, or do the aims of society for the students they teach demand more than this? Why not offer a balance of training and development opportunities over teachers' entire careers that also address their moral purposes, motivation, and self-efficacy? Should not the principles of differentiation, coherence, progression and continuity, and fitness for purpose apply as much to teachers' as to students' learning?

For many decades, visionary educators have sought to develop schools that they believed would be more effective, more productive, more efficient, and oriented toward serving the needs of a diverse population. The contemporary descriptor for these efforts is "reform." However, reality indicates that we are living in a society where change mythology is more apparent than change reality (Georgiades, 1991, p. 106). The standard vocabulary of educators consists of words and phrases such as continuous progress, team teaching, flexible scheduling, individualized instruction, differentiated staffing, cooperative learning, mastery learning, curriculum packages, inclusion, and school effectiveness. Both research and practice show that in most cases change is, indeed, a myth. First, policies for educational change often fail to take into account the central mediating role of school leaders and teachers, and, second, they ignore the importance of attending to both their cognitive and emotional intelligence. Thus, visions of schools that are committed to the education of the whole child become clouded by notions of effectiveness that are limited by social control ideologies, "market forces," and technical efficiency.

During the last two decades, many strategies and models have been implemented for the purpose of raising standards through improving teaching and learning: standard setting, criteria- and norm-referenced assessment, professional development, organizational development, curriculum development, school improvement, school reform networks, effective schools, decentralization of governance and management, and restructuring. It is not difficult to add other examples to this impressive list of "innovations." It is more difficult, however, to evaluate these strategies and models in terms of their effectiveness and efficiency. We tend to plant numerous trees of innovation and then cut them down if they have not rooted fast enough (Freiberg, 1997). In many cases there is no sustained effort. One-shot, single strategies that are developed to overcome problems within the existing, failing educational system come and go (Day, van Veen, & Walraven, 1997; van Veen, 1998). The education system was built primarily

• To serve the upper third of the student body that will go on to further academic or professional education,

• To tolerate another third that will stay in school but learn little of much benefit to them after graduation, and

• To fail at least a third of the student body that initially came there to learn (Lanier, 1997).

Comprehensive, systematic, and long-term approaches—renewal programs grounded in a changing concept of education and schooling—are often lacking. More important for our discussion here, associated efforts to improve teacher education and professional development of teachers that recognize the complexity of teaching and teachers' roles are an exception to the rule (Day, van Veen, & Sim, 1997).

THE COMPLEX NEEDS OF TODAY'S YOUTH

The current need for more comprehensive, integrated approaches in policy and practice in schools with diverse student populations is due in part to the failure of fragmented, provision-oriented approaches. Especially in urban areas, alternative approaches have to be developed because schools and other institutions cannot meet the complex needs of today's youngsters (Wehlange et al., 1989; van Veen, Day, & Walraven, 1998). A significant proportion of the school population is not going to succeed without massive changes in the way that they are educated, supported, and cared for. This problem is much easier to frame than are the structures and strategies for its solution. If children are to become successful members of society, we need new arrangements for the use of community resources. Many urge that, to be more effective, human services institutions in urban environments need to be restructured to complement and coordinate the assistance that schools provide children and families.

In the major cities where problems of schooling are extreme, the critical limits for providing high-quality education would seem to have already been passed (Schorr & Schorr, 1988, and Forsyth & Tallerico, 1993). Absenteeism among both teachers and students is high, and the facilities for ethnic and cultural minority groups in secondary education are extremely limited. These young people are much more likely to leave school without graduating and run a relatively high risk of being unemployed. In Europe, the youth unemployment rates among some ethnic and cultural minority groups are actually above 50 percent. For large numbers of young people education clearly does not perform its function. The overriding picture is one of worsening student problems, burnt-out or disillusioned teachers, and school systems under pressure. In many cities it is difficult to find qualified teachers willing to work in "at risk" schools.

The reality is that most schools are not designed to accommodate the developmental and educational needs of contemporary youth, nor are teachers prepared to deal with these needs (Ponte & van Veen, 1994). Some students learn regardless of the environment we present them, and others drop out if the school doesn't fit. Sometimes schools are not the right place to deliver learning experiences, and, because they are not ready for their clients, blame failure on the parents, the children, and society in general. In these circumstances sometimes dropping out of school is a positive step toward a better future and a trigger for school improvement. There is a lot to be learned from alternative educational approaches for school dropouts (Louwersheimer and van Veen, 1993). Many of these approaches include notions similar to the ones Maslow described more than 35 years ago.

WHAT CAN EDUCATORS DO?

Contemporary schools and teacher preparation programs in most European countries are not responsive to the educational needs of all students.

We need to redesign them with cognizance of the enormous complexity of the new roles and responsibilities of teachers: the persons at the heart of all educational change (O'Hair & Odell, 1995; Day, 1997b). Yet important questions about the kinds of leadership and policy that are needed in schools in the 21st century and the relationships among them need to be addressed if educational excellence and equity are to be achieved. We need ambitious, systematic change strategies, knowing that marginal projects or piecemeal changes will not make the difference. Leaders and policymakers need to know why education is stuck in the past, before they can face the enormous challenges of the future.

We are not optimistic. The history of past efforts to change education has not informed contemporary decisions makers. It is easy to criticize the role of higher education, too, and the meager research and development investments that remain disconnected from education policymakers and practitioners, who themselves concentrate only on fixing the problems of the current system (Day, 1996). Furthermore, many European universities give short shrift to the study of teaching and learning, and remain isolated from teacher preparation and continuing professional development programs. Creation, adoption, and dissemination of innovations is slowed in part because the future education workforce enters the field prepared only to carry on business as usual. Teaching is not only unready for the 21st century, but it is stalled in the early 20th century (Day, 1997a). The challenge requires partnerships and new institutional alignments and, above all, sustained leadership for high-quality educational renewal (Goodlad, 1993 & 1994). The promising concept of Professional Development Schools has to be implemented and sustained. These institutions have the potential to build a new infrastructure for combining research and development with the preparation of future teachers and the professional development of experienced teachers, leaders, and policymakers (Darling-Hammond, 1994).

There are some important lessons to be learned about educational excellence and equity:

- We must invest in teaching and teacher education as intellectual work with moral purposes, and teachers as reflective practitioners as well as expert pedagogues.
- Teachers and teacher educators need sound professional development programs that relate to the learning and motivation needs of students, tak-

ing into account the environments in which they live.

• Teachers need time to engage, routinely, in self-evaluation and con-tinuing professional development over the span of their careers through organizational arrangements and new technologies if they are to sustain a vision of teaching that includes but goes beyond the technical delivery of curriculum content.

• Schools and their communities must form dynamic, sustained con-nections based upon the building of mutual respect and understanding.

• Policymakers must listen more carefully to the messages of research.

Indeed, we would put our money on capacity-building partnerships be-tween schools, communities, and universities. Learning teachers are key to the transformation of schools. Better schools require better teachers! Thus, in order for teachers to lead or co-lead reform efforts, they need both to receive the opportunity and assume the responsibility for expanded pro-fessional development. As the International Conference on Education in Geneva recommended in 1996, we need to design comprehensive policies for teacher education. This recommendation touches, once more, the need for expanding partnerships (1) that serve children, youth, families, and at-risk schools through interprofessional collaboration and service in-tegration, and (2) that facilitate the development of a more responsive, cooperative learning environment (Day, van Veen, & Walraven, 1997).

DOES MASLOW HAVE A MESSAGE FOR EDUCATORS TODAY?

In current educational practice we find little expression of Maslow's ideas and ideals. The atmosphere, the social climate, in many schools to-day is unhealthy. In inner-city schools, in addition to the inequity and ra-cial isolation, children and youth are alienated from learning. The support systems in school for children and youngsters are very often inadequate (van Veen & van der Wolf, 1994). Furthermore, teachers, principals, and paraprofessionals have been neglected. Teachers have become isolated professionals, and schools have developed into isolated social institutions. Teachers cannot work alone. They have to divide the pain and multiply the pleasure. By participating in professional learning communities, teach-ers can extend their understandings, repertoires, and influence, and learn to apply a range of instructional strategies to meet their students' needs within a vision of what could be rather than an acceptance of what is. The need for a social infrastructure that supports growth, learning, and development at the individual and organizational level is paramount.

Nevertheless, teachers and teacher educators may take some encouragement from Maslow's writing. Though his focus was on creating a growth and self-actualization psychology, he does, indirectly, touch upon matters of fundamental importance to teachers and students, teaching and learning. (However, his treatment of "self-actualization," "need," and flawed hierarchical conceit are rightly subject to criticism elsewhere in this volume, and need to be more securely located in knowledge of how contexts influence growth.) His work continues to remind us, for example, that because teachers are in the business of change, they must not only understand its processes but also its purposes and consequences for themselves as well as others. To invest in change, as teachers do every working day of their lives, requires considerable courage, clarity of purpose, emotional fortitude, and intellectual labor. They must be continuing learners, for change demands self-knowledge in varying circumstances, knowledge of others, and also the continuing use of discretionary judgment, which lies at the heart of their work in the classroom. Vision, autonomy, and self-confidence in this sense are, therefore, not options, but essential requirements of good teaching.

Finally, Maslow's work reminds us, if reminders are needed, that teaching and learning are complex and demanding processes that need teachers who are more than technically competent, who are more than operatives who "deliver" the curriculum. He reminds us to value teachers not only for the job they do, but for the job they *can* do in connecting the student's past and present contexts and their possible futures through their ideals, values, hopes, and fears. Maslow reminds us that if we are to invest in our children's futures, we must invest in teachers.

References

Darling-Hammond, G. (1994). *Professional development schools: Schools for developing a profession*. New York: Teachers College Press.

Day, C. W. (1996). The role of higher education in the professional development of teachers: Threat or challenge? In A. F. D. van Veen & W. Veugelers (Eds.),

Vernieuwing van leraarschap en lerarenopleiding (*Innovating teaching and teacher education*) (pp. 23–45). Leuven/Apeldoorn: Garant Publishers.

Day, C. (1997a). Teachers in the twenty-first century: Time to renew the vision. In A. Hargreaves and R. Evans (Eds.), *Beyond educational reform: Bringing teachers back in.* Buckingham: Open University Press.

Day, C. (1997b). Working with the different selves of teachers: Beyond comfortable collaboration. In Hollingsworth, S. (Ed.), *International action research: A casebook for educational reform.* London: The Falmer Press.

Day, C., van Veen, A. F. D., & Sim, W. K. (Eds.) (1997). *Teachers and teaching international perspectives in school reform and teacher education.* Leuven/Apeldoorn: Garant Publishers

Day, C., van Veen, A. F. D., & Walraven, G. (Eds.) (1997). *Children and youth at risk and urban education: Research, policy and practice.* Leuven/Apeldoorn: Garant Publishers.

Forsyth, P. B., & Tallerico, M. (Eds.). (1993). *City schools leading the way.* Newbury Park, CA: Corwin Press.

Freiberg, H. J. (1997). Personal communication to authors.

Geelen, H., van Veen, A. F. D., & Walraven, G. (1996). *Service integration for children and youth at risk in the Netherlands. A special report for the Organisation for Economic Co-operation and Development on Multi-Disciplinary Training.* Utrecht: Sardes.

Georgiades, W. (1991). A dream of tomorrow's school, today. In C. Reavis (Ed.), *The ecology of successful schools. One approach to restructuring* (pp. 106–112). San Antonio: The Watercress Press.

Goodlad, J. I. (1993). School-university partnerships and partner schools. *Education Policy, 7*(1), 24–39.

Goodlad, J. I. (1994). *Centers for educational renewal.* San Francisco: Jossey Bass.

Jackson, P. W. (1968). *Life in classrooms.* New York: Holt, Rineheart and Winston.

Louwersheimer, F. L., & van Veen, A. F. D. (1993). Voor de dag komen. Dagbehandeling niet-schoolgaande jeugd. [*Youth care and intensive day programmes for school drop-outs*]. Utrecht: SWP.

Maslow, A. H. (1962). "Some basic propositions of a growth and self-actualization psychology." In A. W. Combs (Ed.), *1962 ASCD yearbook, Perceiving, behaving, becoming: A new focus for education* (pp. 34–49). Alexandria, VA: Association for Supervision and Curriculum Development.

O'Hair, M. J., & Odell, S. J. (Eds.) (1995). *Educating teachers for leadership and change.* Thousand Oaks, CA: Corwin Press.

Ponte, P., & van Veen, A. F. D. (1994). (Eds.). Intensieve leerlingbegeleiding. School-strategieen in het voortgezet onderwijs. [*Intensive schoolcounseling and guidance. School strategies in secondary education*]. Leuven/Apeldoorn: Garant Publishers.

Schorr, L. B., & Schorr, D. (1988). *Within our reach: Breaking the cycle of disadvantage.* New York: Anchor.

van Veen, A. F. D. (1998). Aanval op schoolverzuim en schooluitval. [*Reversing the cycle of educational failure. Innovative projects in cities and local policy planning.*] Leuven/Apeldoorn: Garant Publishers.

van Veen, A. F. D., & van der Wolf, J. C. (1994). Het onderwijs onder druk. Op weg naar algemene en specifieke leerlingbegeleiding in het voortgezet onderwijs [General and specific forms of school counseling and guidance in secondary education]. In P. Ponte & A. F. D. van Veen (Eds.), Intensieve leerlingbegeleiding. Schoolstrategieen in het voortgezet onderwijs. Leuven/Apeldoorn: Garant Publishers.

van Veen, A. F. D., Day, C., & Walraven, G. (1998). *Multi-service schools: integrated services for children and youth at risk*. Leuven/Apeldoorn: Garant Publishers.

Wehlange, G. G., Rutter, R. A., Smith, G. A., Lesko, N., & Fernandez, R. R. (1989). *Reducing the risk: Schools as communities of support*. London: Falmer.

A Perceptual View
of the Adequate Personality

Arthur W. Combs

This chapter originally appeared in the 1962 ASCD Yearbook, *Perceiving, Behaving, Becoming: A New Focus for Education*.

A Perceptual View of the Adequate Personality

Arthur W. Combs • *University of Florida*

There are two ways we may approach the question of what it means to be a truly healthy, adequate, self-actualizing person. We may attempt to describe what such people are like or we can seek to discover the dynamics of how such people get to be that way. Each of these approaches is, of course, important to our understanding of such people. To provide the professional worker in human relations fields with effective guides for action, however, we need to know particularly the nature of the processes producing adequate personalities. When we understand these "causes," we may be in a favorable position to establish the conditions by which an increasing number of persons can be helped to achieve richer, more satisfying lives.

There are a number of ways in which the problems of causation might be approached. My own favored frame of reference is to view these problems from a perceptual orientation. Perceptual psychologists have stated, as a basic axiom, that all behavior is a product of the perceptual field of the behaver at the moment of action. That is to say, how any person behaves will be a direct outgrowth of the way things seem to him at the moment of his behaving. To change behavior in this frame of reference requires that we understand the nature of the individual's perceptual field. Knowing the meanings that exist for a particular person, we may then be able to create the conditions which will facilitate changes in his behavior and personality.

Looking at the problem from this frame of reference, I will attempt, in the pages to follow, to describe the truly adequate, self-actualizing person in terms of his characteristic way of seeing himself and the world. How do such persons see themselves and the world in which they live? What is the nature of their perceptual organization and how does this differ from their less fortunate fellows? I have sought the answers to these questions in psychological research and theory, on the one hand, and from my own experience as counselor, teacher, and observer of human relations, on the other. In the course of this study I find myself brought back repeatedly to four characteristics of the perceptual field which always seem to underlie the behavior of truly adequate persons. These characteristics are: (a) a positive view of self, (b) identification with others, (c) openness to experience and acceptance, and (d) a rich and available perceptual field.

A POSITIVE VIEW OF SELF

Extremely adequate, self-actualizing persons seem to be characterized by an essentially positive view of self. They see themselves as persons who are liked, wanted, acceptable, able; as persons of dignity and integrity, of worth and importance. This is not to suggest that adequate people never have negative ways of regarding themselves. They very well may. The total economy of such persons, however, is fundamentally positive (Allport, 1955). They see themselves as adequate to deal with life. As Kelley has put it, they see themselves as "enough." Adequate persons have few doubts about their own worth and value and have so large a reservoir of positive regard that negative perceptions are unable to distort the totality. They seem able to say, when it is so, "Yes, I have not been as honest, or fair, or good as I should have been," without such self-perceptions destroying the remainder of the personality structure. Negative aspects of self can be taken in stride. Indeed, it is even this essentially positive structure of self that seems to make *possible* the admission of negative self-references.

When we describe the truly adequate person as seeing himself in essentially positive ways, we are speaking of the individual's self-concept, not his self-report. We mean by the self-concept, the ways in which an individual characteristically sees himself. This is the way he "feels" about himself. The self-report, on the other hand, refers to the way in which an individual *describes* himself when he is asked to do so. These are by no means identical (Benjamins, 1950). What a person *says* he is and what he *believes* he is may be very far apart. Indeed, the person who finds it most necessary to claim a positive self may even turn out to be the least adequate. When we describe the adequate personality as feeling essentially positive about himself, it is his self-concept we are talking about, not his self-report. It is what he *feels* about himself, not what he says of himself, that determines his behavior.

We are beginning to discover that the kind of self-concepts an individual possesses determines, in large measure, whether he is maladjusted or well adjusted (Combs, 1952). For example, it is not the people who see themselves as liked, wanted, acceptable, worthy, and able who constitute our major problems. Such people usually get along fine in our culture and make important contributions both to themselves and to the societies in which they live. It is the people who see themselves as unliked, unwanted, unworthy, unimportant or unable who fill our jails, our mental hospitals, and our institutions. These are the maladjusted; the desperate ones, against whom we must protect ourselves, or the defeated ones, who must be sheltered and protected from life. It is the people who feel inadequate, who succumb to brainwashing, who feel so little faith or strength within themselves that they are fair game for any demagogue who offers security and strength from without. The movement toward personality health is an expression of increased strength of self, just as bodily health is the product of strength of physique (Goldstein, 1939). Psychotherapists have repeatedly observed that improvement in mental health is correlated with a stronger, more positive view of self (Rogers & Dymond, 1954).

Positive View of Self Expressed in Action

A positive view of self gives its owner a tremendous advantage in dealing with life. It provides the basis for great personal strength. Feeling positively about themselves, adequate persons can meet life *expecting* to be successful. Because they expect success, they behave, what is more, in ways that tend to bring it about. "The rich get richer and the poor get poorer" (Eriksen, 1954). With such a basic security, life can be met straightforwardly. Courage comes naturally. Indeed, behavior which seems courageous to their fellows often to very adequate people seems to be only the "normal" thing (Maslow, 1954).

Because they feel essentially sure about themselves, self-actualizing persons can feel a higher degree of respect for their own individuality and uniqueness. As a consequence they are less disturbed or upset by criticism (Brownfain, 1952). They can remain stable in the midst of stress and strain. Positive feelings of self make it possible to trust themselves and their impulses. They can utilize themselves as trustworthy, reliable instruments for accomplishing their purposes. They have less doubts and hesitation about themselves. Small wonder that weaker persons are often drawn to them or that adequate people are likely to gravitate into leadership roles (Benjamins, 1950)

With a self about which he can be fundamentally sure, a person is free to pay much more attention to events outside the self (Bills, 1953). When the house is in good shape and food is set by for the winter, one is free to go adventuring. A strong self can be forgotten on occasion. A weak self must be forever buttressed and cared for. It intrudes in every situation. With a strong self, problems can be dealt with more objectively because self is not at stake. Solutions can be sought solely as "good" answers to the problem at hand, rather than in terms of their immediate contribution to the enhancement of self. Adequate persons can afford to behave unselfishly because the self is already basically fulfilled.

An essentially positive view of self permits adequate people to be effective without worry about conformity or nonconformity. For them, conformity is not a goal or even a way of dealing with life, but only an artifact of the process of problem solving. They can behave in terms of what seems best to do, and let the chips fall where they may. When the goal is problem solution without the necessity for personal aggrandizement, then, whether one conforms or not is merely an outsider's judgment of what happened, not a governing motivation in the behaver.

Having a positive view of self is much like having money in the bank. It provides a kind of security that permits the owner a freedom he could not have otherwise. With a positive view of self one can risk taking chances; one does not have to be afraid of what is new and different. A sturdy ship can venture farther from port. Just so, an adequate person can launch himself without fear into the new, the untried, and the unknown. This permits him to be creative, original, and spontaneous. What is more, he can afford to be generous, to give of himself freely or to become personally involved in events (Maslow, 1954). Feeling he is much more, he has so much more to give.

Development of a Positive Self

The self-concept, we know, is learned. People *learn* who they are and what they are from the ways in which they have been treated by those who surround them in the process of their growing up. This is what Sullivan called "learning about self from the mirror of other people" (Sullivan, 1947). People discover their self-concepts from the kinds of experiences they have had with life; not from telling, but from experience. People develop feelings that they are liked, wanted, acceptable, and able from *having been* liked, wanted, accepted, and from *having been* successful. One learns that he is these things, not from being told so, but only through the experience of *being treated as though he were so*. Here is the key to what must be done to produce more adequate people. To produce a positive self, it is necessary to provide experiences that teach individuals they are positive people.

It is a common fallacy among many lay people and some teachers that, since the world is a very hard place and people sometimes fail, children should be introduced to failure early. The logic of this position, at first glance, seems unassailable and in harmony with the goal of education to "prepare for life." But the position is based on a false premise. Actually, the best guarantee we have that a person will be able to deal with the future effectively is that he has been essentially successful in the past. People learn that they are able, not from failure, but from success. While it may be true that toughness and adequacy come from successfully dealing with problems, the learning comes not from experiencing failure but from successfully avoiding it. Similarly, to feel acceptable one must experience acceptance. To feel lovable one must have been loved. A positive view of self is the product of fulfillment, of having been given. The product of deprivation is a diminished self, and even, if carried to extreme, a depraved self.

IDENTIFICATION WITH OTHERS

A second major characteristic of the truly adequate personality seems to be his capacity for identification with his fellows. The self-concept, we know, is not confined to the limits of the physical body alone. It is capable of contraction or expansion so that the self may be defined so narrowly as to virtually exclude the physical body or expanded so greatly as to include many other people and things. Psychologists have pointed out that infants are highly egocentric and only with growth and maturity achieve an increasing degree of altruism. Some people, unfortunately, never achieve such feelings and remain to the end of their days capable of concern for little more than their own welfare. Others, among them the most adequate men and women in history, seem to reach a point where they can identify with great blocks of mankind, with *all* mankind, without reference to creed, color, or nationality. Truly adequate people have a greatly expanded feeling of self.

This feeling of oneness with their fellows does not mean that adequate personalities are necessarily charming hosts or hostesses or even that they like to be surrounded with people. We are not talking of "togetherness" or a frantic need to be with people. Identification has to do with a *feeling* of oneness with one's fellows. This feeling can exist without demanding that a particular individual be a "hail fellow well met" or "life of the party." It is even conceivable that he might not like parties or might prefer to spend much of his time alone in individual pursuits. Searching for a new cure for cancer all alone in a laboratory, for example, may be a profound demonstration of concern for others.

The feeling these truly adequate persons have has also been described as a feeling of "belonging." Unfortunately, this term has come to mean, for some people, "joining," being a member of, or "keeping up with the Joneses." The feeling of belonging characteristic of these adequate people is a far cry from that. It is a feeling of unity or oneness, a feeling of sharing a common fate, or of striving for a common goal. It represents a real extension of the self to include one's fellows.

Expression of the Feeling of Identification

The feeling of oneness with one's fellows produces in the truly adequate person a high degree of responsible, trustworthy behavior. There is reason for this response. When identification is strong, one cannot behave in ways likely to be harmful or injurious to others, for to do that would be to injure one's self. As a consequence, adequate persons are likely to manifest a deep respect for the dignity and integrity of other people and a strong sense of justice and moral probity. A self which truly encompasses others is incapable of "selfishness," in the usual sense. This is a kind of enlightened selfishness in which the boundaries between self and others disappear. One cannot behave in ways which ignore and reject others when self and others are one. It should not surprise us, therefore, that adequate persons usually possess a deep sense of duty or responsibility or that they are likely to be democratic in the fullest sense of the word (Combs & Snygg, 1959).

The feeling of identification also seems to produce a deep sensitivity to the feelings and attitudes of others. The motives of adequate persons are much more likely to be others-centered (Phillips, 1951). Pity and compassion are far more a part of their daily lives and experience. Warmth and humanity come easily to these people as a logical outgrowth of their feeling of oneness with their fellows. This sensitivity also finds its expression in what Maslow has described as a "non-hostile sense of humor" (Maslow, 1954).

Because they have strong feelings of identification, adequate persons can work harmoniously with others in either a leader or follower role (Bell & Hall, 1954). Feeling adequate, they do not *have* to lead in order to prove their strength and power. Leadership for them is not a way of proving superiority, but a way of organizing to accomplish desirable ends. The feeling of identification produces such trust in others that adequate persons can lead or not as the situation demands and be satisfied in either role.

How Identification Is Acquired

Identification, like the self-concept, is learned. It is the product of the individual's experience and an outgrowth of the essentially positive view of self we have already described. One learns to identify with others, depending upon the nature of his contacts with the important people in his life. As people are friendly and helpful, it is easy and natural to extend one's self to include them or to feel at one with them. As people are harmful and rejecting, on the other hand, one's need to protect himself produces an organization from which such people must be excluded. It is a natural reaction to build walls against those who hurt and humiliate us. On the other hand, it is possible to lower defenses when we can be sure of the friendly behavior of others.

Truly adequate people are able to go further. They can often identify even with those who are antagonistic to them. To do this requires that one feel so strong within himself as to be confident he can withstand the attacks of others. The insecure self can identify only with those who make him feel safe and secure. The more positive the individual's feelings about self, the easier it is to identify with an ever broader sample of mankind. The capacity for identification appears to be a product of an essentially positive view of self and of successful, satisfying experiences in interaction with other people. Here is a place where a child's experiences in school can be made to count.

OPENNESS TO EXPERIENCE AND ACCEPTANCE

Truly adequate persons possess perceptual fields maximally open to experience. That is to say, their perceptual fields are capable of change and adjustment in such fashion as to make fullest possible use of their experience. Truly healthy persons seem capable of accepting into awareness any and all aspects of reality (Rogers, 1947, 1957). They do not find it necessary to defend themselves against events or to distort their perceptions to fit existing patterns. Their perceptual fields are maximally open and receptive to their experiences.

This capacity to confront life openly and without undue defensiveness has sometimes been called acceptance. Acceptance, however, should not be confused with resignation. The openness to experience we are describing refers to the ability to admit evidence into awareness. One cannot deal effectively with what he is unable to conceive exists. The admission of evidence to awareness is the first necessary step to effective action. Being willing to confront the facts, however, does not mean one is defeated by them. On the contrary, it is the only basis upon which any action can safely be premised.

The capacity for acceptance is directly related to the individual's freedom from the experience of threat (Taylor & Combs, 1952). We know that when people feel threatened: (a) their perceptions become narrowed to the threatening events, and (b) they are forced to the defense of their existing perceptual organizations. These unhappy concomitants of threat are the very antithesis of the openness to experience we have been describing as characteristic of the truly adequate personality. Whether an individual feels threatened, furthermore, is a product of two factors we have already discussed; namely, the positive self and identification. The more secure the individual's self, the less he will feel threatened by events and the more open he can be in relating to the world about him. Similarly, the more the individual is identified with other people, the less threatened he will feel by those who surround him and the more he will be able to accept his experience with others with equilibrium and profit. Openness to experience and acceptance, it thus appears, are related to the individual's freedom from threat, and this freedom in turn is a product of positive self and identification.

To this point we have spoken of the adequate person's acceptance of events outside himself. But the openness to experience and acceptance we have been describing refer equally to the individual's perceptions of self. Adequate persons are more accepting of themselves (Vargas, 1954). Feeling fundamentally positive about self makes it less necessary to be defensive or to bar from perceptual organization what is true about self. Adequate persons are less likely to be at war with themselves and so see themselves more accurately and realistically.

Effect of Acceptance upon Behavior

A greater openness to experience offers many advantages. It provides adequate people with more data and, with more data, they are much more likely to be right. Maslow found, for example, that his self-actualizing people were not only connatively right, they were cognitively right as well (Maslow, 1954). A more open perceptual field can encompass more. Adequate people are thus more likely to include the generic as well as the specific aspects of problems or to perceive events or details that would be missed or would seem unimportant to others. This is another way of saying adequate persons behave more intelligently, for what else is intelligence but the ability to behave more effectively and efficiently?

A broader, more accurate perception of the world permits adequate persons to behave more decisively. Decisions can be made with more certainty when one feels he is in command of the data and feels sufficiently sure of self to be unafraid to commit himself to action. Decisions made on the basis of more data are likely to be better ones. On the other hand, the straightforward, uncomplicated relationship these people have with reality also makes it possible for them to live comfortably *without* a decision when this is called for. They are characterized by what Frenkel-Brunswik (1949) called a "toleration of ambiguity." That is, they find it possible to live comfortably with unsolved problems. They do not *have* to have an answer when there is none yet, so are less likely to adopt spurious or expedient explanations.

The accurate, realistic assessment of self resulting from acceptance makes possible the use of self as a dependable, trustworthy instrument for achieving one's purposes. These people do not kid themselves. They can permit themselves to be what they are while working to become the best they can be. They do not have to fight what they are. As a consequence, they are free to devote their energies to what is positive and constructive. With a more accurate conception of self, they can and do set more realistic goals for themselves (Child & Whiting, 1949; Cohen, 1954; Friedenberg & Roth, 1954). Their levels of aspiration are more likely to be in line with their capacities. Because goals are more realistic, they are more likely to achieve them. And, of course, the more often goals are achieved, the more positively they feel about self and the more acceptance of and openness to experience become possible for them.

Increased capacity to accept self, we know, permits greater acceptance of others as well (Berger, 1952; McIntyre, 1952; Sheerer, 1949). Adequate people are, therefore, less disturbed and upset by the errors and transgressions of their fellows. They are able to take them, too, as they are. They can be more sympathetic and less judgmental. Because they do not demand of others that they be what they are not, they can have greater patience and forbearance in dealing with human foibles. With a greater openness to and acceptance of other people, human relationships are likely to be more successful, since they derive from broader, more accurate perceptions of what other people are like. Disillusionment and despair in human relationships are the product of inaccurate assessment of what people are like and what can be expected of them. A clear conception of possibilities and limitations is more likely to produce more realistic goals. These in turn provide the bases for success experience and good morale.

The capacity for openness to experience and acceptance makes life more pleasant and exciting for adequate persons. It permits them to feel a greater wonder and appreciation of events (Maslow, 1954). Without the necessity for defensiveness, the world can be met openly and gladly. Life can be experienced and savored without fear or hesitation. It can be lived "to the hilt." Such people experience more of what Maslow has called "peak experiences." What is more, adequate persons seem to remain more imaginative and creative even when well along in years.

Dynamics of Openness and Acceptance

Openness and acceptance are not innate characteristics. They are learned. Adequate persons develop these capacities as a function of an essentially positive self and identification. An essentially positive self and a strong feeling of identification with one's fellows make it possible for adequate persons to operate freer from the inhibiting and crippling effects of the experience of threat (Chodorkoff, 1954). What contributes to the child's feelings of security and integrity and to his feelings of oneness with his fellow human beings makes possible a greater acceptance of and openness to his experience.

A third factor contributing to acceptance of and openness to experience is the existence of a value system that prizes openness. Perceptual psychology has presented us with a vast body of research demonstrating the effect of values on the perceptual field. It seems clear that persons who have developed attitudes of valuing new experience, of seeking personal growth, or of the testing of idea against idea are likely to develop perceptual fields more open and accepting. Values of this sort, moreover, can be learned and can be taught. The individual's search for personal adequacy can end, as it does for many, in attempts to protect the precious self, to ring it round with defensive works and to reject or ignore what might cause disruption or change (Lecky, 1945). Or, fulfillment may be found in an approach to life which flirts with danger, actively seeks for challenge, enjoys the testing of one's mettle or the satisfaction of achieving a new goal or objective. The kind of experience provided to people in their most formative years will determine which kinds of values they espouse.

Acceptance is learned. Clinical evidence shows that children can accept even the most formidable handicaps if these handicaps can be accepted by those who surround them. Accurate, realistic concepts of self are essential bases for growth and fulfillment and are in turn the products of one's experience. It is characteristic of the neurotic that he is unable to accept either himself or his fellows. In the protocols of psychotherapy one can perceive how neurotics reject themselves and their associates. It is apparent in these protocols, too, that as clients get better, they become increasingly able to accept themselves and the people and events which surround them (Conrad, 1952; Hartley, 1951; Rogers, 1947; Rogers & Dymond, 1954; Sheerer, 1949; Vargas, 1954). Apparently one learns to accept himself and others as a function of having *experienced* acceptance. It is not surprising, therefore, that modern psychotherapy stresses the acceptance of the client by the therapist as an essential for progress. But the experience of acceptance is by no means limited to the relationship of therapist and client. Acceptance can be experienced in the relationships of the child with his family, his peer group or his teachers in the public schools.

A RICH AND AVAILABLE PERCEPTUAL FIELD

To this point we have described the adequate personality in terms of his perceptions of self, of others, and of the openness of the perceptual field to experience. In the complex society in which we live one cannot be both adequate and stupid simultaneously. The truly adequate person must also be well informed. Indeed, the minimum level of what everyone needs to know just to exist continues to rise year by year as we become ever more specialized and dependent upon technical know-how. One need not know everything to be adequate, but one must certainly have a field of perceptions, rich and extensive enough to provide understanding of the events in which he is enmeshed and available when he needs them. Adequate people have such perceptual fields.

This does not mean that their perceptions are necessarily of an abstract, intellectual character or gained solely from formal schooling. Rich perceptual fields may be derived from quite informal sources through firsthand involvement in human relations, in business, in recreation, or in performing a trade or occupation. On the other hand, with the rapid rise of specialization and technology in our world, perceptions of a technical and abstract character become increasingly necessary for successful action and are less and less available from informal sources. Whatever their origin, however, the fields of adequate people are rich and extensive.

The mere existence of perceptions within the perceptual field is not enough, however, to assure effective behavior. We have already observed that the fields of adequate people are open to their experience. This facilitates the development of a rich and extensive field. The richest field, however, is of little account unless perceptions are available when they are needed for action. This availability, too, seems characteristic of the fields of adequate persons. They not only possess more information or understanding; they are more able to produce these when needed and to put them to effective use.

Some Effects of a Rich and Available Perceptual Field

Clearly, if behavior is a function of perceptions, then a rich and available perceptual field makes possible more effective, efficient behavior. One can do a better job when he has a fine array of tools immediately at hand than he can when he is limited to the use of a hammer and screw driver for every task no matter what its character. Just so, with wider choices open to them, adequate persons can and do operate in ways more satisfying and productive both for themselves and for the world in which they live. They show better judgment and are more often right in their observations and decisions. This is simply another way of saying they behave more intelligently (Combs, 1952).

How Rich and Available Fields Are Acquired

People get their perceptions, we have seen, as a consequence of their experience. Rich and extensive perceptual fields are a product of the kinds of opportunities an individual has been exposed to. Other things being equal, the richer the opportunity, the more likely the development of a rich and extensive field. It is such opportunities that educators have long sought to provide for children. Unfortunately, other things are seldom equal and, as any teacher is aware, mere exposure to an event is no guarantee that the event will be perceived by the individual or be available on later occasions.

Something more than confrontation with events is necessary to insure inclusion of perceptions in the field and their availability on later occasions. This availability seems dependent upon at least two factors: (a) the individual's discovery of personal meaning, and (b) the satisfaction of need.

The degree to which any perception will affect behavior depends upon its personal meaning for the individual. Perceptions may exist at any level of meaning—from isolated bits of information that pass through our consciousness, like the bits of news we read at the foot of a newspaper column, to those perceptions having deep personal meanings for us, like our feelings about a daughter or son, or those concerned with matters in which we are deeply interested, as a business project, hobby, or the like. These varying levels of personal meaning are expressed in the words we use to describe such perceptions. Arranged in order of increasing meaning, we speak, for example, of looking, seeing, knowing; of understanding, belief, conviction. The deeper, more personally significant the perception, moreover, the more likely it is to affect behavior.

Adequate people seem to have many more such personal meanings. As a consequence, much more of their knowing affects behaving. They are less easily swayed and much more precise and efficient because the relationship and pertinence of perceptions are clearer and more available when needed. Such meanings, of course, are a result of the nature of the individual's experience. One learns the meaning of events. Whether perceptions exist as isolated knowings or as deep personal understanding will depend upon the opportunities, stimulation, and encouragement a person has had, the values he has acquired, the freedom he has had to explore and discover meaning, and the existence of a positive self.

The availability of perceptions in the field will also be vitally affected by the individual's achievement of need satisfaction. Need has a focusing effect upon perception. We perceive what we *need* to perceive. A more adequate self permits attention to wander far afield from self while the inadequate person, desperately seeking maintenance and enhancement of self, must, of necessity, focus most of his perceptions on events contributing directly to such feelings. Failure of need satisfaction produces narrowness and rigidity of perceptual organization. The adequate individual, on the other hand, with a secure self, has a more fluid, open field of perceptions. It follows, then, that the production of a more available field requires the development of a positive view of self, and a positive self, we have already seen, is a function of the kinds of experiences provided in the course of a child's maturing.

In this paper I have attempted to describe the truly adequate, healthy person in terms of four characteristics of the perceptual field: a positive view of self, identification with others, acceptance of and openness to experience, and the richness and availability of the perceptual field. Since all of these ways of perceiving are learned, they can also be taught if we can but find ways to provide the necessary kinds of experiences. No other agency in our society is in a more crucial position to bring about these necessary conditions than are the public schools. Indeed, the production of such people must be the primary goal of education.

To contribute effectively to the production of such persons, however, is not as much a question of revolution as it is of evolution. To produce adequate persons requires not that we do something entirely new and different, but that we all do more efficiently and effectively what some of us now do only sometimes and haphazardly. Educators have been in the business of effecting changes in perception since teaching was invented. No one knows better than they how to bring such changes about. Our new understandings of the truly healthy personality provide us with new and important objectives toward which to direct our efforts. Who can say what kind of world we might create if we could learn to increase our production of adequate people?

Selected References

Allport, G. W. (1955). *Becoming: Basic considerations for a psychology of personality*. New Haven, CT: Yale University Press.

Bell, G. B., & Hall, H. E., Jr. (1954). The relationship between leadership and empathy. *Journal of Abnormal and Social Psychology, 49*, 156–157.

Benjamins, J. (1950). Changes in performance in relation to influences upon self-conceptualization. *Journal of Abnormal and Social Psychology, 45*, 473–480.

Berger, E. M. (1952). The relation between expressed acceptance of self and expressed acceptance of others. *Journal of Abnormal and Social Psychology, 47*, 778–782.

Bills, R. E. (1953). Attributes of successful educational leaders. In: R. L. Hopper (Ed.), *Interdisciplinary research in educational administration*. Lexington, KY: College of Education, University of Kentucky Press.

Brownfain, J. J. (1952). Stability of the self-concept as a dimension of personality. *Journal of Abnormal and Social Psychology, 47*, 597–606.

Child, I. L., & Whiting, J. W. M. (1949). Determinants of level of aspiration: Evidence from everyday life. *Journal of Abnormal and Social Psychology, 44*, 303–314.

Chodorkoff, B. (1954). Self-perception, perceptual defense, and adjustment. *Journal of Abnormal and Social Psychology, 49*, 508–512.

Cohen, L. D. (1954). Level-of-aspiration behavior and feelings of adequacy and self-acceptance. *Journal of Abnormal and Social Psychology, 49*, 84–86.

Combs, A. W. (1948). Phenomenological concepts in non-directive therapy. *Journal of Consulting Psychology, 12*, 197–208.

Combs, A. W. (1952). Intelligence from a perceptual point of view. *Journal of Abnormal and Social Psychology, 47*, 662–673.

Combs, A. W., & Snygg, D. (1959). *Individual behavior: A perceptual approach to behavior* (Rev. ed.). New York: Harper & Brothers.

Combs, A. W., & Soper, D. W. (1957). The self, its deviate terms and research. *Journal of Individual Psychology, 13*, 134–145.

Conrad, D. (1952). An empirical study of the concept of psychotherapeutic success. *Journal of Consulting Psychology, 16*, 92–97.

Eriksen, C. W. (1954). Psychological defenses and "ego strength" in the recall of completed and incompleted tasks. *Journal of Abnormal and Social Psychology, 49*, 45–50.

Frenkel-Brunswik, E. (1949). Distortion of reality in perception and social outlook. *American Psychologist, 4*, 253.

Friedenberg, E. Z., & Roth, J. A. (1954). *Self-perception in the university: A study of successful and unsuccessful graduate students.* Chicago: University of Chicago Press.

Goldstein, K. (1939). *Organism: A holistic approach to biology derived from pathological data in man.* New York: American Book Co.

Hartley, M. (1951). *Changes in the self-concept during psychotherapy.* Unpublished doctoral dissertation, University of Chicago.

Lecky, P. (1945). *Self-consistency: A theory of personality.* (J. F. A. Taylor, Trans. & Ed.). New York: Island Press.

Maslow, A. H. (1954). *Motivation and personality.* New York: Harper & Brothers.

McIntyre, C. J. (1952). Acceptance by others and its relation to acceptance of self and others. *Journal of Abnormal and Social Psychology, 47*, 624–625.

Phillips, E. L. (1951). Attitudes toward self and others: A brief questionnaire report. *Journal of Consulting Psychology, 15*, 79–81.

Rogers, C. R. (1947). Some observations on the organization of personality. *American Psychologist, 2*, 358–368.

Rogers, C. R. (1957). *The concept of the fully functioning person* (Mimeographed statement). University of Chicago.

Rogers, C. R., & Dymond, R. F. (Eds.). (1954). *Psychotherapy and personality change: Coordinated research studies in the client-centered approach.* Chicago: University of Chicago Press.

Sheerer, E. T. (1949). An analysis of the relationship between acceptance of and respect for self and acceptance of and respect for others in ten counseling cases. *Journal of Consulting Psychology, 13*, 169–175.

Sullivan, H. S. (1947). *Conceptions of modern psychiatry.* Washington, DC: William Alanson White Psychiatric Foundation.

Taylor, C., & Combs, A. W. (1952). Self-acceptance and adjustment. *Journal of Consulting Psychology, 16,* 89–91.

Vargas, M. J. (1954). Changes in self-awareness during client-centered therapy. In C. Rogers & R. Dymond (Eds.), *Psychotherapy and personality change: Co-ordinated research studies in the client-centered approach.* Chicago: University of Chicago Press.

Other Publications by the Author

Combs, A. W. (1957, February). The myth of competition. *Childhood Education, 34,* 119–128.

Combs, A. W. (1958). Seeing is behaving. *Educational Leadership, 16,* 21–27.

Combs, A. W. (1959). Personality theory and its implications for curriculum development. In A. Frazier (Ed.), *Learning more about learning* (pp. 5–20). Washington, DC: Association for Supervision and Curriculum Development.

Combs, A. W., & Snygg, D. (1959). *Individual behavior: A perceptual approach to behavior* (Rev. ed.). New York: Harper & Brothers.

A Response to

"A Perceptual View of the Adequate Personality"
by Arthur W. Combs

What Does Recent Research Say About the "Truly Adequate Person"?

Hermine H. Marshall • *San Francisco State University, San Francisco, California*

For the 1962 ASCD Yearbook, Arthur Combs wrote the chapter "A Perceptual View of the Adequate Personality" from the perspective of perceptual psychology. He based his work on the premise that the goal of education is to develop "a truly healthy, adequate, self-actualizing person" (p. 119). Combs postulated four characteristics of the way fully functioning individuals see themselves and the world—characteristics of their perceptual field: "(a) a positive view of self [including beliefs about uniqueness, worth, and importance, as well as expectations for success], (b) identification with others, (c) openness to experience and acceptance, and a rich and available perceptual field" (p. 120).

Combs's objective was to suggest the processes and contributing factors through which we might achieve the educational goal of developing "truly adequate" individuals.

In this chapter, I focus on research over the past two decades concerning the processes and factors underlying these characteristics—primarily those contributing to a positive view of self and identification with others—that will help us meet Combs's educational goal, particularly in a culturally diverse society. First, I present recent research from a variety of perspectives that has supported and elaborated on Combs's ideas and their

Note: References to Arthur Combs's 1962 chapter reflect the page numbers of the chapter as reprinted in this book (pp. 117–135).

136

underlying processes.[1] Second, I describe areas where recent research and educational theory have suggested expanding Combs's framework. Finally, I comment on the role of culture in creating meanings in an increasingly diverse society.

SUPPORT AND ELABORATION FOR COMBS'S IDEAS

Research has supported and elaborated on the ways schools, parents, and communities can enhance the development of "truly adequate" individuals. Let's examine three areas of influence:

- The role of expectations for success,
- The negative effects of the self-focused actions of those having a weak sense of self, and
- Factors that influence identification with and sympathy for others.

Expectations

Combs pointed out that adequate people expect success and behave in ways that lead to success. Their positive feelings, beliefs, and ways of behaving result from how these individuals were treated as they grew up.

Research conducted in the 1980s and 1990s has elaborated on how teachers and parents contribute to students' expectations for success. For example, in some classrooms, students perceive teachers treating high and low achievers differently. These students interpret these differences in teacher treatment as indicating different expectations and act on these interpretations, resulting in different levels of achievement (e.g., Brattesani, Weinstein, & Marshall, 1984; Jussim & Eccles, 1992). Teachers, therefore, need to be sensitive to factors that convey expectations for success so that expectancy messages are not conveyed differently according to students' ability level (Marshall & Weinstein, 1986), gender (Meece & Eccles, 1993), race (Graham, 1984), or other cultural or linguistic characteristics. Teachers need to convey expectations that all students can succeed and that they can learn strategies to attain success.

---

[1]Barbara McCombs describes other supports for Combs's work (this volume, pp. 148–157).

Research has shown that parental expectations have similar effects. For example, mothers' gender-role stereotypes influence mothers' beliefs about their sons' and daughters' ability in math and social fields. These beliefs, in turn, influence their children's self-perceptions. In fact, research has found mothers' perceptions to be a more powerful influence on children's self-perceptions than teacher ratings (Jacobs & Eccles, 1992). Consequently, educators need to be concerned also with helping parents understand the effects of their expectations on their children's success.

Counterproductive Self-Focused Actions

Recent research also supports Combs's view that people who lack a strong sense of self often engage in counterproductive self-focused actions. Covington (1984), Elliott and Dweck (1988), and others have conducted extensive research on the differences between students who are motivated to learn and master material and students who are motivated to protect their own egos.

For example, students with a *learning orientation* are more likely to use metacognitive and deep-processing strategies (like trying to figure out how new information fits with what is already known) that facilitate learning and effective problem solving (e.g., Nolen, 1988). In contrast, those with an *ego-protective orientation* are more likely to use superficial strategies (like copying and guessing) or failure-avoidance strategies, such as not trying (because failing after making an effort indicates low ability, and low ability is less valued in our culture). By using these strategies, students who lack a positive view of their abilities can preserve a superficial image of being capable, but in reality fail to gain understanding.

To overcome the detrimental effects of self-focused actions, Clifford (1984) has suggested helping such students attribute their lack of success to a lack of appropriate strategies, rather than to concerns about their perceived level of ability. Teachers need, therefore, to help students understand that it is not perceived ability but use of effective strategies that affects success in school. At the same time, teachers need to focus on the exact areas where the student is having a problem, then teach new strategies to overcome that problem. When students learn new strategies (such as monitoring comprehension or identifying main ideas) and then attribute their consequent success to effective strategies, they have a chance to surmount the problem and gain new motivation to learn (see also Borkowski, Carr, Rellinger, & Pressley, 1990).

Identification with Others

In *Perceiving, Behaving, Becoming,* Combs stated that self-actualizing individuals have the ability to "identify with . . . *all* mankind, without reference to creed, color, or nationality" (p. 124, italics in original). These people have a positive and broadly encompassing view of self; and, as a result, they are more likely to display compassion, have a strong sense of justice, and behave unselfishly. According to Combs, this capacity appears to evolve from satisfying experiences with others, including those at school.

Recent research also supports this contention. Eisenberg (1992) summarizes research findings that cross-cultural differences in altruism, at least toward members of their own group, were related to nurturance and support, responsibility for chores contributing to family well-being, and cultural values. These results are consistent with Combs's ideas. Similarly, within cultures, some of the factors influencing prosocial values and behavior are valuing and modeling generosity and caring by significant others, as well as warm, supportive relationships with parents.

This finding is exemplified by a comparison of rescuers of Jews from Nazi oppression in Germany with nonrescuers. A critical difference between these two groups was learning to be more inclusive in their view of those to whom they felt ethical obligations. Similar views were found in those most committed to the civil rights movement in the 1960s. Interestingly, the *parents* of people committed to preserving the lives and dignity of those less fortunate played a primary role by emphasizing that moral principles applied to all human beings. Compared to nonrescuers, rescuers also reported that their parents used reasoning rather than physical discipline. Parents of rescuers, as well as the parents of committed civil rights workers, lived their beliefs and modeled caring in their interactions with those outside their families as well.

Although a close family bond may facilitate modeling, this research suggests the importance of both parents' and teachers' altruistic values and behavior. Through professional development for teachers and parent education, more teachers and parents could learn to encourage empathy by their own behavior, as well as by using disciplinary techniques that stress reasoning rather than punishment or reinforcement.

Educators have developed curriculum materials and school-based programs to promote this goal. For example, the Child Development Project (Battistich, Solomon, Watson, & Schaps, 1997) has developed a school-based program designed to encourage support and caring. This program emphasizes the importance of prosocial and democratic values, autonomy and self-direction, working collaboratively, and personal responsibility and understanding. Research has shown that the program promotes a caring community, as well as prosocial values, regardless of the economic level of the school. The Consistency Management & Cooperative Discipline Program similarly incorporates themes of caring, cooperation, and community (Freiberg, this volume, pp. 56–57).

IDEAS THAT NEED RECONSIDERATION AND EXPANSION

Recent research has suggested a reconsideration of some of Comb's ideas, such as (a) the relationship between global views of self and self-concept in specific domains, (b) cultural influences on conceptions of self, and (c) the framework within which these processes occur.

Global Versus Specific Domains of Self and Self-Concept

For Combs, self-concept means "the ways in which an individual characteristically sees himself" (p. 120). This seems to imply a global self-perception. Combs also referred to specific aspects of self, such as competence and virtue; but he did not address the relationship between global perceptions of self and perceptions in specific domains.

Combs's concern with a positive view of self is reflected in continued research on global self-worth.[2] In addition, in the past 15 years, researchers

---

[2]Combs distinguished between *self-report,* which refers to the way people describe themselves when asked, and *self-concept,* which refers to what a person actually believes about himself or herself. Most research on self-concept has been conducted with self-report questionnaires. Nevertheless, since the results of this research are often linked to behavior—and the link to behavior seems to define Combs's view of self-concept—these methods may very well reflect beliefs about self.

have explored the existence of components of self in a manner beyond that identified in Combs's chapter. For example, researchers like Harter (1996) and Marsh, Byrne, and Shavelson (1988) have examined several dimensions within self-concept, such as academic, social, and physical self-concept (and self-esteem). They have also explored subdimensions of academic self-concept including those reflecting competence in school subjects, such as math self-concept and verbal self-concept. These researchers have also investigated some hypotheses about the development of a differentiated and hierarchically structured view of self and its relationship to global self-worth and to success.

In his 1962 work, Combs had little to say about two other aspects of self-perception: ethnicity and gender. Recent research concerning relationships between self-esteem and ethnic identity has shown inconsistent results. These relationships are complex and affected by many other factors, including the strength, salience, and meaning of an individual's ethnic or racial identity, as well as the status of and discriminatory attitudes toward particular groups within the larger society (Phinney, 1996). These factors cannot be ignored in considering how to enhance a positive view of self.

We know more today about gender differences. Girls are more likely to underestimate and boys more likely to overestimate their academic and physical abilities, particularly as they reach adolescence. Further, girls with feminine self-identities are more likely to have low perceived academic competence (academic self-concept).[3] On the other hand, researchers have found that girls hold more positive perceptions of their social competence. Despite these differences in girls' and boys' perceptions of social competence compared with academic and physical competence, some research shows no gender differences in generalized perceptions of competence (Phillips & Zimmerman, 1990). It may be that positive views of self in the social arena compensate for a lack of positive self-perceptions in these other domains.

Although boys and girls may show no differences in global self-worth, the effects of stereotypes and negative perceptions of academic and physical competence continue to limit girls' success in these domains. Thus, it

---

[3]Several researchers (e.g., Harter, 1996; Phillips & Zimmerman, 1990) have used the term *perceived competence* when referring to individuals' self-concept of ability in particular areas.

appears that global self-worth needs to be supported by positive views of self in specific domains to achieve full functioning, an idea not considered in Combs's chapter.

Other research on the relationship between global self-worth and self-perceptions indicates that when a person considers certain domains important—such as social acceptance or academic competence—those domains are highly correlated with global self-esteem (Harter, 1996). For elementary and middle school children, dimensions of physical attractiveness and social acceptance dominate a global sense of self-worth to a greater extent than cognitive competence or behavior.[4] These findings suggest a concern with the role of the media, as well as that of families and schools, in influencing self-regard. Research also underscores the role of classroom atmosphere, by showing the importance of peer groups, such as classmates, in determining self-worth.

Influence of Culture

A second area where research has also moved beyond Combs's notions of self concerns differences across cultures in conceptions of self. Combs's description of a positive view of self includes beliefs about the dignity, integrity, uniqueness, worth, and importance of each individual. Recently, Markus and Kitayama (1991) have contrasted this familiar Western "independent" view of self with an "interdependent" view of self more common in many Asian cultures, as well as African, Latin American, and some southern European cultures. This interdependent conception of self emphasizes harmony in attending to and fitting in with others, rather than the uniqueness and individuality that Westerners consider important.

Although Combs recognized the importance of views of self that include "great blocks of mankind" (p. 124), the interdependent view seems different, for example, in that it does not include an emphasis on the uniqueness and importance of each individual. In essence, our Western view of self does not seem adequate to describe the views of some other cultures.

---

[4]The dominance of physical appearance seems to continue into adulthood (Harter, 1996).

According to an interdependent view, self is a part of nature, not separate from it. In contrast to the Western view of the self, the Eastern view is that the self and significant others are interconnected. In the interdependent view, significant others are included *within* the self—yet these connections change as social contexts change. A person's self-esteem is determined in part by fulfilling obligations to and being a part of various interpersonal relationships. Individuals within this system are motivated to respond to the needs and demands of others, rather than to satisfy their own needs.

Further, researchers have found variation both within and between cultures. We need to recognize this variation as we reconsider the essence of a fully functioning person within a culturally diverse society. As we attempt to enhance the self-concepts of those we teach, we need to include a broader conception of the meaning of self that incorporates alternative cultural views. This more inclusive view needs to become a part of our rich and available perceptual field. The self as unique and separate does not seem to be a universal value, and we can all benefit from an understanding of self-in-relation-to rather than separate-from others and nature.

Social Constructivist and Sociocultural Frameworks

Finally, we might find it productive to expand Combs's framework by supplementing the perceptual psychology framework with a greater understanding of the social and cultural factors that contribute to the conception of truly healthy people.[5] As Combs noted, perceptual psychology emphasizes the individual's construction of personal meanings. This view seems consistent with what is referred to as a *constructivist* view, particularly a cognitive constructivist view.

In contrast, *social constructivism* emphasizes the role of *social interaction* through which socially shared meanings, knowledge, and contexts are constructed (Marshall, 1992, 1996). According to a social constructivist framework, learning and thinking are developed in *social* interaction rather than being solely a result of personal meaning construction (see also

---

[5]These few paragraphs cannot do justice to the richness of these theories. The references listed in this article provide further information on social constructivist and sociocultural perspectives.

Vygotsky, 1978; Wertsch, 1985). Through active participation with others, people create socially shared meanings for what is of value, for how to be an adequate person within the culture, for what it means to be a student within a particular classroom, and for what the meanings of academic content are. In addition, although other frameworks recognize social context as a given background factor, social constructivists see the social context itself as being continually constructed in dynamic and ongoing interactions among the participants. The opportunities provided for learning within a culture and within a classroom are examples of contexts that are socially constructed (e.g., Collins & Green, 1992).

A helpful way of integrating personal and social processes may be derived from Rogoff's (1995) *sociocultural* approach. She proposes that three planes are involved simultaneously: community, interpersonal, and personal:

- On the *community* plane, people actively participate with others in "culturally organized activities" that provide cultural and situational supports and constraints. These culturally organized and influenced activities include child-rearing practices, schools, and apprenticeships.

- On the *interpersonal* plane, social partners (including parents, teachers, and peers), as well as the cultural and social values of the community, guide the participation of learners either explicitly or tacitly, for example, in how to become involved in a classroom that functions as a community of learners (e.g., Collins & Green, 1992).

- On a *personal* plane, individuals change through their involvement in culturally organized activities, including family and classroom activities. They become involved in developing mutually shared meanings, although these meanings and subsequent behaviors are constrained by the particular culture and situation.

Rogoff's concepts are useful in placing Combs's views into a larger sociocultural perspective that educators need to consider, particularly as our society becomes more diverse.

TOWARD TRULY ADEQUATE INDIVIDUALS IN A MULTICULTURAL SOCIETY

Combs concludes his 1962 chapter by referring to "new understandings of the truly healthy personality" (p. 133) and how these kinds of understanding may direct our educational efforts toward a better world. Since his chapter was written, we have gained enhanced understanding from research that supports and expands Combs's views. This research also provides clues for nourishing fully functioning individuals. In addition, we have achieved a richer understanding by becoming aware of the role that culture plays in creating meanings and in supporting and constraining behavior. These new understandings inspire us to recognize alternative conceptions of what it means to be a truly adequate, fully functioning person within a culturally diverse society.

If we are to have an expanded understanding of multiple meanings created by differences among cultures and individuals, we will need to be open to new experiences and ways of thinking, supplemented by a rich and available perceptual field—the last two characteristics of a self-actualizing individual as noted by Combs.

References

Battistich, V., Solomon, D., Watson, M., & Schaps, E. (1997). Caring school communities. *Educational Psychologist, 32,* 137–151.

Borkowski, J., Carr, M., Rellinger, E., & Pressley, M. (1990). Self-regulated cognition: Interdependence of metacognition, attributions, and self-esteem. In B. F. Jones & L. Idol (Eds.), *Dimensions of thinking and cognitive instruction* (Vol. 1, pp. 53–92). Hillsdale, NJ: Erlbaum.

Brattesani, K., Weinstein, R., & Marshall, H. (1984). Student perceptions of differential teacher treatment as moderators of teacher expectation effects. *Journal of Educational Psychology, 76,* 236–247.

Clifford, M. (1984). Thoughts on a theory of constructive failure. *Educational Psychologist, 19,* 108–120.

Collins, E., & Green, J. (1992). Learning in classroom settings: Making or breaking a culture. In H. H. Marshall (Ed.), *Redefining student learning: Roots of educational change* (pp. 59–86). Norwood, NJ: Ablex.

Combs, A. W. (1962). A perceptual view of the adequate personality. In A. W. Combs (Ed.), 1962 ASCD yearbook, *Perceiving, behaving, becoming: A new focus for education* (pp. 50–64). Alexandria, VA: Association for Supervision and Curriculum Development.

Covington, M. (1984). The motive for self-worth. In R. Ames & C. Ames (Eds.), *Research on motivation in education* (Vol. 1, pp. 78–114). New York: Academic Press.

Eisenberg, N. (1992). *The caring child.* Cambridge, MA: Harvard University Press.

Elliott, E., & Dweck, C. (1988). Goals: An approach to motivation and achievement. *Journal of Personality and Social Psychology, 54,* 5–12.

Graham, S. (1984). Communicating sympathy and anger to black and white children: The cognitive (attributional) consequences of affective cues. *Journal of Personality and Social Psychology, 47,* 14–28.

Harter, S. (1996). Historical roots of contemporary issues involving self-concept. In B. Bracken (Ed.), *Handbook of self-concept: Developmental, social, and clinical considerations* (pp. 1–37.) New York: John Wiley.

Jacobs, J., & Eccles, J. (1992). The impact of mothers' gender-role stereotypic beliefs on mothers' and children's ability perceptions. *Journal of Personality and Social Psychology, 63,* 932–944.

Jussim, L., & Eccles, J. (1992). Teacher expectations II: Construction and reflection of student achievement. *Journal of Personality and Social Psychology, 63,* 947–961.

Markus, H., & Kitayama, S. (1991). Culture and the self: Implications for cognition, emotion, and motivation. *Psychological Review, 98,* 224–253.

Marsh, H., Byrne, B., & Shavelson, R. (1988). A multifaceted academic self-concept: Its hierarchical structure and its relation to academic achievement. *Journal of Educational Psychology, 80,* 366–380.

Marshall, H. H. (1992). Seeing, redefining, and supporting student learning. In H. H. Marshall (Ed.), *Redefining student learning: Roots of educational change* (pp. 1–32). Norwood, NJ: Ablex.

Marshall, H. H. (1996). Recent and emerging theoretical frameworks for research on classroom learning: Contributions and limitations. *Educational Psychologist, 41* (Special Issue).

Marshall, H. H., & Weinstein, R. (1986). Classroom context of student-perceived differential teacher treatment. *Journal of Educational Psychology, 78,* 441–453.

Meece, J., & Eccles, J. (1993). Special feature: Gender and educational achievement. *Educational Psychologist, 28,* 313–405.

Nolen, S. (1988). Reasons for studying: Motivational orientations and study strategies. *Cognition and Instruction, 5,* 269–287.

Phillips, D., & Zimmerman, M. (1990). The developmental course of perceived competence and incompetence among competent children. In R. Sternberg & J. Kolligian, Jr. (Eds.), *Competence considered* (pp. 41–66). New Haven, CT: Yale University Press.

Phinney, J. (1996). When we talk about American ethnic groups, what do we mean? *American Psychologist, 51,* 918–927.

Rogoff, B. (1995). Observing sociocultural activity on three planes: Participatory appropriation, guided participation, apprenticeship. In A. Alvarez, P. Del Rio, & J. V.

Wertsch (Eds.), *Sociocultural studies of mind* (pp. 139–164). Cambridge, UK: Cambridge University Press.

Vygotsky. L. (1978). *Mind in society: The development of higher psychological processes.* Cambridge, MA: Harvard University Press.

Wertsch, J. (1985). *Vygotsky and the social formation of mind.* Cambridge, MA: Harvard University Press.

A Response to

"A Perceptual View of the Adequate Personality" by Arthur W. Combs

What Role Does Perceptual Psychology Play in Educational Reform Today?

Barbara L. McCombs • *Mid-continent Regional Educational Laboratory, Aurora, Colorado*

I have the honor of reviewing a timeless and profound work by Arthur W. Combs: "A Perceptual View of the Adequate Personality," published in the 1962 ASCD Yearbook, *Perceiving, Behaving, Becoming*. In this chapter, Combs linked concepts from perceptual psychology to education—resulting in what he called "person-centered education." In the process, he identified the qualities of effective helpers (for example, counselors or teachers), and he defined the assumptions that need to underlie educational reform. What do these ideas mean for education today? Are they still relevant in standards-based, achievement-oriented, content-focused educational reform?

Art Combs is my "neighbor." He lives in Greeley, Colorado, where he is a professor emeritus of education at the University of Northern Colorado—a short distance from my home in Denver. I've had the benefit of talking with him about his ideas and seeing how his work is continuing to influence our thinking about what schools should and could be. My comments in this review reflect my discussions with Art, and I feel strengthened in my belief that his ideas are even more relevant to educators today than they were more than 35 years ago.

As well as being a primary contributor to the 1962 ASCD Yearbook, Art Combs served as Chair of the 1962 Yearbook Committee. In talking

Note: References to Arthur Combs's 1962 chapter reflect the page numbers of the chapter as reprinted in this book (pp. 117–135).

about that experience with me, he said that in creating the theme of the book, the committee wanted to focus educators on the goal of helping students develop healthy personalities. Committee members believed this goal was vital to all living systems, from the individuals themselves to the systems that support them (e.g., family, school, community). With the growing evidence that characteristics of a healthy personality are not innate but can be learned (and changed), Combs continues to believe that schools play a critical role in developing these characteristics in students and in teaching them how they can be maintained throughout life.

WHAT CHARACTERISTICS CAN SCHOOLS HELP DEVELOP?

According to Combs (1962), schools need to create the kinds of experiences that will effect the changes in perceptions necessary to produce truly adequate, healthy people. Combs has spent a considerable part of his life exploring person-centered, perceptual approaches and qualities of effective helpers in the fields of teaching, counseling, social work, pastoral care, and clinical psychology. For example, he reported 13 studies that clearly revealed that the common qualities of effective helpers are "a direct outcome of the helper's perceptual organization or belief system. It is what the helper believes that makes the difference" (Combs, 1986, p. 55).

Learner Characteristics

In Combs's (1962) view, the truly adequate person (1) has a positive view of self, (2) identifies with others, (3) is open to experience and acceptance, and (4) has a rich and available perceptual field. I talked with him in March 1997, and he further emphasized that helping learners at all levels of the system to learn new perspectives related to positive functioning and outcomes is a far simpler process than attacking complex external factors or behavior (Combs, 1997). He explained that the aim of this internal learning process in any living system—from the individual to the organizational level—is to clarify beliefs about what's important. For example, how do you view yourself and others, and how much freedom—or how much control—is appropriate for the person or the organization?

As we talked about these ideas and their evolution since 1962, Combs explained that "person-centered education" had encountered resistance in the fields of psychology and education. He described how basic principles of learning from perceptual psychology that had been known since the 1940s were being ignored in favor of behavioral and mechanistic models that put the focus on external factors such as rewards and punishments. He expressed frustration at how long it has taken for educators to accept perceptual ideas. But he also said he was optimistic about current perspectives in education—including constructivism, social constructivism, systems thinking, and brain research. He was encouraged that all these approaches to education emphasize connections, relationships, and fields of meaning that surround us and promise to transform our thinking and our systems to better serve the needs of all (see also Combs, Miser, & Whitaker, 1999).

Teacher Characteristics

Art and I talked about my recent work in helping teachers understand their beliefs and assumptions about learning, learners, and teaching, as well as their perceptions of classroom practices relative to individual students. I relayed how we have rediscovered the strength of perceptions for producing motivation and learning—in students and teachers alike. From our work (McCombs, 1997; McCombs & Whisler, 1997) on learner-centered principles and practices (i.e., the Learner-Centered Model) with more than 10,000 middle and high school students and their more than 1,000 teachers—we have identified the beliefs common to the most effective teachers within a learner-centered model:

• They believe in their competency to be an effective teacher and facilitator of learning for all students.

• They believe that they can influence student learning even during the difficult stage of adolescence.

• They believe in the influence of thoughts and feelings on actions and tend to analyze and reflect on personal or professional experiences.

• They believe that they should not control learning but provide support for student choice and personal control over learning.

• They believe that all learners are capable of learning, that learning is a process of constructing personal meaning, and that teaching is a process of facilitating students' natural learning and motivational processes.

Furthermore, effective teachers perceive that their practices create positive interpersonal relationships and classroom climate, honor student voice, provide individual learning challenges, encourage student perspective taking, encourage higher-order thinking and self-regulated learning, and adapt to a variety of individual and developmental student differences.

Verification of these qualities also comes from students themselves. For example, when students are asked about the qualities of "good" teachers, they report that they are more committed to learn with teachers who have the following qualities:

• They enjoy teaching both students and the subject.
• They make lessons interesting and relevant to life outside school.
• They are fair and open.
• They are easy for students to talk to.
• They are comfortable with laughing but know how to keep order.
• They explain things without making students feel "small."
• They don't shout.
• They don't give up on students.
• They don't go on about matters that discredit students (Rudduck, Day, & Wallace, 1997).

According to Combs and his person-centered, perceptual view of education, teachers and schools need to help students learn healthy ways of thinking about themselves and others—not just in school but for a lifetime.

COMMON DENOMINATORS UNDERLYING
DESIRED CHARACTERISTICS

From my analysis of the person-centered, perceptual perspective, two common denominators underlie the process of becoming an adequate person today: (1) transformed beliefs and (2) transformed actions and behavior. Both involve *learning and change* as central to the process of becoming an adequate person. They are also based on current knowledge of how learning occurs and the nature of the learning process as a change in thinking and behaving (cf., APA, 1993, 1997).

Transformed Beliefs

Learning fundamentally different ways of thinking and perceiving self and others defines a transformational process that is central to the person-centered, perceptual view of education. Combs (1991) maintains that to truly change our public schools, we must focus on changing the ways people think, work, and affect each other.

Consistent with this view, many researchers (cf., McCombs & Whisler, 1997; Rudduck et al., 1997) are verifying that accomplishing these changes requires helping both teachers and students "change their minds" or modify their current thinking. We need to help teachers learn to value what students think about school and classroom practices. Then teachers and students can negotiate positive strategies and collaborate to define changes in practice and expectations. When beliefs change, classroom practices and school climate change; and students can experience more positive expectations, higher motivation, and higher achievement.

Transformed Actions and Behavior

In understanding the complex and pervasive influence of people's thinking in creating their actions, Combs (1991) has observed that when educators' assumptions are person centered, such a focus does not imply a prescription for particular teaching strategies or practices. How teachers implement "person-centered education" may vary widely from school to school and class to class. As we have found in our work with the Learner-Centered Model, classroom practices need not take a particular form or look a particular way.

When teachers transform their actions and behavior, however, they see learning as a natural process and focus on the conditions that best support this process for all students. In interactions with students, teachers must ensure that they

- Include learners in educational decision-making processes, whether in relation to their learning or classroom rules.
- Encourage and regard the diverse perspectives of students during learning.
- Account for and respect the differences of learners' cultures, abilities, styles, developmental stages, and needs.
- Treat learners as co-creators in the learning process, as individuals with ideas and issues that deserve attention and consideration (McCombs & Whisler, 1997).

In our work with schools using the Learner Centered Model, we have also focused on what we call "will, skill, and social support." Within this model, *will* is an innate or "self-actualized" state of motivation, an internal state of well-being, in which people are in touch with their natural self-esteem, common sense, and intrinsic motivation to learn. *Skill* is an acquired cognitive or metacognitive competency that develops with training and practice. *Social support* is the enabling, person-centered context for the empowerment of will and development of skill. Social supports include quality relationships and interactions with others. The key point is that this model embodies the person-centered, perceptual view: It begins with an acknowledgment of the centrality of thinking to actions.

WHAT DOES THE PERCEPTUAL VIEW CONTRIBUTE?

It is apparent to me that Combs's person-centered, perceptual view of education is consistent with what we have learned about learning from constructivist and social constructivist theories. In fact, I believe that perceptual psychology was ahead of its time. That is, it recognized that schools must acknowledge, respect, and help people build meaning from personal perceptions. And it also recognized that *schools must deal with meaning and personal perceptions, not just provide facts.* If schools are to make a difference in children's lives, educators must bring the "facts" into each child's world of "meaning." Recent research is extending perceptual psychology and person-centered education into two areas: (1) student perceptions and the role of student voice and (2) fundamental principles underlying "living systems."

Acknowledging Learner Perspectives and Voices

The work of Rogers and Freiberg (1994) exemplifies the power of attending to student perspectives in defining schools where students love to learn. When the researchers asked students what motivates them to learn in school, they consistently reported that they want

- To be trusted and respected.
- To be part of a family.
- Their teachers to act as helpers.
- Opportunities to be responsible.
- Freedom, not license.
- A place where people care.
- Teachers who help them succeed, not fail.
- To have choices.

Other researchers (McCombs & Lauer, 1997) have also shown that student perceptions about their instructional experiences and their beliefs about themselves as learners are the best predictors of motivation and academic achievement in school.

Understanding Living Systems

A person-centered, perceptual view is implicit in the work of many visionaries who are arguing that the current system cannot be restructured; it must, they maintain, be transformed (e.g., Senge, 1990; Wheatley & Kellner-Rogers, 1996). Complex living systems, such as education, that function to serve particular human needs are by their nature unpredictable. But we can understand complex systems in terms of the following:

- Principles that define human needs.
- Cognitive and motivational processes.
- Variabilities of behavior.

Unlike nonliving systems, living systems demand that we focus on interconnectedness, self-renewal, and interdependence. When we tinker with one component of the system, we influence all others. Implied in this view is a more global, nonlinear, and dynamic view of learning and change

(Banathy 1997). Living systems conform to basic psychological and socio-logical principles that define people and their interactions with others; thus, we are better able to understand complex living systems by under-standing psychological and sociological principles.

In systemic school reform, the focus turns to people, their thinking, and the interrelationships among them. Combs and the other contributors to the 1962 Yearbook initiated this focus by emphasizing a person-centered, perceptual approach to education.

WHERE NEXT?

The tension between a focus on the learner and a focus on what is learned is still apparent in today's educational reform agenda—with its emphasis on facts, content, and high achievement of standards. Those of us with a person-centered, perceptual view acknowledge that an emphasis on what students should learn is necessary, but insufficient, if our goal is for people to find personal meanings in what they learn. Today, the perceptual view of education continues to point us to the person—not only to what people learn and how they learn it—but to each learner and his or her unique perceptions, meanings, and needs. In discussing what educational reform needs, Combs (1991) argues that without a change in our basic as-sumptions, reforms go round and round the same loops, forever refining the status quo.

Reform efforts are now centered around the standards movement, which identifies what is important for learners to know and be able to do (McCombs, Whisler, & Lauer, 1997). With this focus, there has been a shift from what we should teach to what learners actually should learn. For example, the usual course plan or syllabus would specify what material should be covered during a semester or year. With the advent to standards-based instruction, what students should know and be able to do in each content area is described and benchmarked for various grade levels (for example, 4th, 8th, 12th). In the area of geography, the two different statements might look like this:

- *Content-based:*   The content to be covered includes differences in the complexity of information available from maps, globes, and other geographical tools that can be used to solve problems.

- *Standards-based:*   The student will evaluate the related merits of maps, globes, and other geographical tools to solve problems.

This shift in focus from *teaching* required content to *learning* valued knowledge and skills, as identified in standards, focuses us on the processes of learning.

From the person-centered, perceptual view, however, this focus goes only part of the distance necessary, if our goal is to educate *all* students. Why? Because without a corresponding focus on individual learners, we are in danger of continuing to ignore students' calls for help when they report feeling disconnected from their teachers and peers, think school is irrelevant, or drop out mentally or physically because they just don't want to be in school.

* * *

In conclusion, I am grateful for this opportunity to verify how valuable a contribution Art Combs's work and the 1962 ASCD Yearbook were and continue to be. This work reminds us of the foundational role of personal meanings, constructed experiences, and person-centered approaches in learning and being. It helps us put standards, content, and achievement in perspective. This work also alerts us to the importance of building on great thinking and thinkers as we connect what we know about people, about learning, and about personal meanings with current constructivist learning theories and the educational reform agenda. I am honored to help us not forget.

References

APA Task Force on Psychology in Education. (1993, January). *Learner-centered psychological principles: Guidelines for school redesign and reform.* Washington, DC: American Psychological Association and the Mid-continent Regional Educational Laboratory.

APA Work Group. (1997, June). *Learner-centered psychological principles: A framework for school redesign and reform.* (Rev. ed.). Washington, DC: American Psychological Association, Board of Educational Affairs, and Board of Scientific Affairs.

Banathy, B. H. (1997). Designing educational systems: Creating our future in a changing world. *Educational Technology, 32*(11), 41–46.

Combs, A. W. (1962). A perceptual view of the adequate personality. In A. W. Combs (Ed.), *Perceiving, behaving, becoming: A new focus for education* (1962 ASCD Yearbook, pp. 50–64). Alexandria, VA: Association for Supervision and Curriculum Development.

Combs, A. W. (1986). What makes a good helper? A person-centered approach. *Person-Centered Review, 1*(1), 51–61.

Combs, A. W. (1991). *The schools we need: New assumptions for educational reform.* Lanham, MD: University Press of America, Inc.

Combs, A. W., Miser, A. B., & Whitaker, K. S. (1999). *On becoming a school leader: A person-centered challenge.* Alexandria, VA: Association for Supervision and Curriculum Development.

McCombs, B. L. (1997). Self-assessment and reflection: Tools for promoting teacher changes toward learner-centered practices. *NASSP Bulletin, 81*(587), 1–14.

McCombs, B. L., & Lauer, P. A. (in press). Development and validation of the Learner-Centered Battery: Self-assessment tools for teacher reflection and professional development. *The Professional Educator, 20*(1), 1–21.

McCombs, B. L., & Whisler, J. S. (1997). *Learner-centered classroom and schools: Strategies for increasing student motivation and achievement.* San Francisco: Jossey-Bass.

McCombs, B. L., Whisler, J. S., & Lauer, P. A. (1997). *Maximizing the effectiveness of standards-based and standards-referenced educational models.* Aurora, CO: Mid-continent Regional Educational Laboratory.

Rogers, C., & Freiberg, H. J. (1994). *Freedom to learn* (3rd ed.). New York: Merrill.

Rudduck, J., Day, J., & Wallace, G. (1997). Student perspectives on school improvement. In A. Hargreaves (Ed.), *Rethinking educational change with heart and mind.* 1997 ASCD Yearbook (pp. 73–91). Alexandria, VA: Association for Supervision and Curriculum Development.

Senge, P. M. (1990). *The fifth discipline: The art and practice of the learning organization.* New York: Doubleday.

Wheatley, M. J., & Kellner-Rogers, M. (1996). *A simpler way.* San Francisco: Berrett-Koehler.

About the Authors

H. Jerome Freiberg is a John & Rebecca Moores University Scholar and Professor of Education in the College of Education at the University of Houston. He is the editor of the *Journal of Classroom Interaction*. He is international director and founder of the Consistency Management & Cooperative Discipline Program. Dr. Freiberg has received the University of Houston's Teaching Excellence Award, the College of Education Award for Teaching Excellence, and the College of Education Senior Research Excellence Award. He is the author of *Universal Teaching Strategies*, 2nd edition, with Amy Driscoll (Allyn & Bacon, 1996), and he revised the 3rd edition of *Freedom to Learn* by the psychologist Carl Rogers (Merrill, 1994). Forthcoming books in 1999 are *Beyond Behaviorism: Changing the Classroom Management Paradigm* (Allyn & Bacon); and *School Climate: Measuring, Improving and Sustaining Healthy Learning Environments* (Falmer Press). He may be contacted at the University of Houston, Room 350, Farish Hall, Houston, TX 77204-5872. Phone: 713-743-8663. Fax: 713-743-8664. E-mail: CMCD@uh.edu

Dottie Bonner is the Magnet Coordinator at Austin High School for Teaching Professions, 1700 Dumble, Houston, TX 77023, and a doctoral student in Curriculum and Instruction at the University of Houston, 4800 Calhoun Rd., Houston, TX 77004. She taught high school English for 18 years, wrote curriculum, and has been in her current position for 8 years. Her primary interest is in teacher recruitment and preparation. Phone: 713-924-1608. Fax: 713-924-1687. E-mail: dbonner@houston.isd.tenet.edu

Arthur W. Combs is a teacher, consultant, and psychologist. In 1947, along with Donald Snygg, he invented perceptual-experiential psychology, a systematic frame of reference for the study of persons. A past president of the Association for Supervision and Curriculum Development, he was the editor of the 1962 ASCD Yearbook, *Perceiving, Behaving, Becoming: A New Focus for Education*. He has written 22 books and monographs and more than 150 articles on psychology, counseling, and education. His most recent books are *Being and Becoming: A Field Approach to Psychology*

(New York: Springer Pub., 1999) and *On Becoming a School Leader: A Person-Centered Challenge*, coauthored with Ann B. Miser and Kathryn S. Whitaker (ASCD, 1999).

Christopher Day, Cert. Ed., M.A., D.Phil., Ph.D. (h.c.), F.R.S.A., is Professor of Education, Head of Humanities Division, and Co-Director of the Centre for Teacher and School Development, Graduate School of the University of Nottingham, University Park, Nottingham N67 2RD, England. He has worked as a schoolteacher, teacher educator, and schools superintendent, and has extensive research and consultancy experience in England, Europe, Australia, Southeast Asia, and North America in the fields of teachers' continuing professional development, action research, leadership, and change. His most recent books are *Developing Teachers: The Challenges of Lifelong Learning* (Falmer Press, 1999) and *Developing Leadership in Primary Schools* (coauthored with C. Hall and P. Whitaker; Paul Chapman Ltd., 1998). He is editor of *Teachers and Teaching: Theory and Practice*, and co-editor of *Educational Action Research* and *Journal of In-Service Education*. Phone: 44-115-9514423. Fax: 44-115-9514435. E-mail: Christopher.Day@nottingham.ac.uk

Carolyn A. Jackson is a counselor at G. C. Scarborough High School, Houston Independent School, 4141 Costa Rica, Houston, TX 77092, and a doctoral student at the University of Houston, Houston, TX 77204. She serves on the board of directors for Phi Delta Kappa (University Park Chapter). She is also a member of Phi Beta Delta (an international honor society). She has also participated in teacher inservices in Sri Lanka. Phone: 713-613-2200. Fax: 713-613-2205. E-mail: CJack44@YaHoo.Com

Earl C. Kelley spent most of his life in education, as teacher, administrator, supervisor, and college professor. He was a consultant to school systems through the United States and wrote extensively about educational problems, sharing his deep understanding of teachers and students. His research into perceptual approaches to understanding human behavior appeared in a number of articles. His books include *Education for What Is Real, The Workshop Way of Learning*, and *Education and the Nature of Man* (coauthored with Marie I. Rasey).

Alfie Kohn writes and speaks widely on human behavior, education, and social theory. He is the author of six books, including *No Contest: The Case*

Against Competition (Houghton Mifflin, 1986; rev. ed., 1992); *The Brighter Side of Human Nature: Altruism and Empathy in Everyday Life* (Basic Books, 1990); *Punished by Rewards* (Houghton Mifflin, 1993); and, most recently, *What to Look for in a Classroom ... and Other Essays* (Jossey-Bass, 1998). Kohn has written five cover articles for *Phi Delta Kappan* as well as contributing to *Educational Leadership, Education Week*, the *Journal of Education*, and many other periodicals. He can be reached at 242 School St., Belmont, MA 02478.

Lawrence Kohn is an English facilitator at Quest High School, 18901 Timbers Forest Dr., Humble, TX 77346. Quest is an Annenberg Challenge Grant Beacon School and a member of the Coalition of Essential Schools in the Humble Independent School District. An educator of 16 years, he received his B.S. in English from Youngstown State University in 1982 and his M. Ed from the University of Houston in 1995. He is currently a research assistant and working toward his Ed. D in Curriculum and Instruction at the University of Houston, College of Education. His dissertation focuses on school reform and restructuring in the United States. Phone: 281-812-3447. Fax: 281-852-3132. E-mail: kohnhead@insync.net

Hermine H. Marshall is Professor of Education at San Francisco State University. She is former associate editor of the *Journal of Educational Psychology* and editor of *Redefining Student Learning: Roots of Educational Change* (Ablex, 1992). Her interests include self-concept and motivation for learning—particularly as these are influenced by classrooms and cultural differences. She may be contacted at 27 Norwood Ave., Kensington, CA 94707. Fax: 510-558-9072. E-mail: hmarshal@sfsu.edu

Abraham H. Maslow was a psychologist, professor, and one of the founders of humanistic psychology. Throughout his life he conducted research and wrote extensively about mental health and human potential, adding to the field such psychological concepts as the hierarchy of needs, self-actualizing persons, and peak experiences. His books include *Toward a Psychology of Being, Motivation and Personality*, and *New Knowledge in Human Values*.

Barbara L. McCombs is Senior Director for the Human Development and Motivation group at the Mid-continent Regional Educational Laboratory (McREL), 2550 S. Parker Rd., Suite 500, Aurora, CO 80014. She has more than 25 years of experience directing research and development efforts in a wide range of basic and applied areas. She is the primary author of *Learning-Centered Psychological Principles: Guidelines for School Redesign and Reform*, disseminated by the American Psychological Association. Under her direction, her group recently completed a professional development program for teachers based on the *Principles*, entitled *FOR OUR STUDENTS, FOR OURSELVES: Putting Learner-Centered Principles into Practice*. Phone 303-632-5537. Fax: 303-752-6388. E-mail: bmccombs@mcrel.org

Norman A. Newberg is a Senior Fellow at the University of Pennsylvania's Graduate School of Education and Executive Director of the Say Yes to Education Foundation. Using an action research methodology, he consults nationally with public and private school systems focusing on school restructuring to maximize articulation and the sharing of student data and human resources across school-level boundaries. For over 10 years he has conducted a longitudinal study of 112 inner-city students from low-income families. Phone: 215-898-1819. Fax: 215-898-1089. E-mail: NormanN@NWFS.GSE.Upenn.edu

Carl R. Rogers was a psychotherapist who originated client-centered therapy and was one of the founders of humanistic psychology. The American Psychological Association bestowed on him its Distinguished Scientific Contribution and Distinguished Professional Contribution Awards. His influence also extended to the fields of education, counseling, conflict resolution, and peace. He was nominated for the Nobel Peace Prize. He wrote more than 200 professional articles and numerous books, including *On Becoming a Person, Client-Centered Therapy*, and *Freedom to Learn*.

Mary R. Sudzina is Associate Professor of Educational Psychology, Department of Teacher Education, University of Dayton, Dayton, OH 45469-0525. She is the author of *Case Study Applications for Teacher Education: Cases of Teaching and Learning in the Content Areas* (Allyn & Bacon, 1999). Her research interests include case-based pedagogy, teaching with technology, and school reform. Phone: 937-229-3389. Fax: 937-229-3199. E-mail: sudzina@udayton.edu

Dolf van Veen is Executive Director of ESAN (the Centre for Educational Collaboration Amsterdam/North Holland) and Director of Research and Innovation of the Amsterdam City Project on School Attendance and Drop-out at the Dienst Welzijn Amsterdam, Weesperstraat 85, 1018 VN Amsterdam, The Netherlands. He is Special Professor at the School of Education, University of Nottingham (England) and Chair of the Research Division on Children and Youth at Risk and Urban Education of the European Educational Research Association. Recent publications include *Multi-Service Schools: Integrated Services for Children and Youth at Risk* (Garant Publishers, 1998), with Christopher Day and Guido Walraven; and *Teachers and Teaching: International Perspectives on School Reform and Teacher Education* (Garant Publishers, 1998), with Christopher Day and Wong-Kooi Sim. Phone: 31-20-617 4052. Fax: 31-20-552-2681. E-mail: veend@dsef01.amsterdam.nl

Please remember that this is a library book,
and that it belongs only temporarily to each
person who uses it. Be considerate. Do
not write in this, or any, library book.

Date Due

MAR 25 2000		
AUG 29 2000		
OC 23 '02		
MY 13 '03		
AP 7 04		
1/1/05		